REYES CÁRDENAS

CHICANO POET
1970-2010

AZTLAN LIBRE PRESS
SAN ANTONIO, TEXAS

First Edition

San Antonio, Texas
210.710.8537
www.aztlanlibrepress.com
editors@aztlanlibrepress.com

Dedicated to the promotion, publication and
free expression of Xican@ Literature and Art

Publishers/Editors:
Juan Tejeda
Anisa Onofre

Veteran@s Series

Cárdenas, Reyes.
Reyes Cárdenas: Chicano Poet 1970-2010
ISBN-10: 0-9844415-5-7
ISBN-13: 978-0-9844415-5-6
1. Poetry 2. Chicano Poetry
3. Mexican-American Poetry. 4. Texas
5. Seguin 6. Chicano Literature

Library of Congress Control Number: 2013931315

Cover Art: *Finally Found Her Chic, After Searching the Universe (The Vato Transformed Himself into a Robot)* © L.A. David.

Chicano artist L.A. David created 11 original title-page black & white illustrations for each of the 11 sections included in this book.

L.A. David was born and raised in S.A., the Westside of San Antonio, Texas, where he exhibited a flair for the visual arts and drawing at an early age. It was at Fox Tech High School where his art and design work flourished, winning several awards. During the late 60s and early 70s he worked with various businesses and organizations as he became involved in the Chicano Movement. He attended San Antonio College where he mingled with different artists and studied art movements such as Impressionism, Cubism, Dadaism, and Pop Art. "At San Antonio College I explored my purpose as an artist," he says, "and had my first one-man show." L.A. David is constantly experimenting with his art and this has led him on a unique, expression-driven explosion of cosmic comic relief as exemplified in his series of colorful neonesque characters and caricatures known as "Los Burros," a humorous exaggeration and eclectic mix of "vatos y vatas" from the barrios who communicate with space aliens and Nahuatl ancestors. They are the individuals in touch with their indigenous and cosmic roots, who have returned from the Planeta Burro — the Ivy League colegios such as Yale, Havard, Princeton — to inspire a younger generation of "burros" in a cool, funky, and far-out way of relating to current issues. Some paintings interpose the Lowrider culture with the burros as a driving force that propels the artwork into socio-political themes. L.A. David says that "los burros are everywhere, their caricatures are only part of a larger landscape of inspiration."

Contact L.A. David at vatobag@yahoo.com

Photo on page prior to Contents: Reyes at about age 10 (ca. 1958), and photos on page 372 (About the Author), and back cover (2013), courtesy of the author.

Photo on page 18: Reyes at about age 23 (ca. 1971), courtesy of César Augusto Martínez.

Minimal editing was done on this book, primarily for spelling and some punctuation. In Reyes' work, he usually spells Aztlán with an accent, as is customary in the Spanish language. In this book we use Aztlan without the accent to honor the original Nahuatl language. Seguín is spelled in context, sometimes with the accent, and sometimes without, to connote its usage in the U.S. Most of the time, lowercase letters are used in the names alurista and raulrsalinas to honor these author's preferred spelling.

ACKNOWLEDGMENTS

One's life work is never an individual effort. Many people have influenced and played a major part in my literary life. Cecilio García-Camarillo and Mia Stageberg created the early me. Carmen Tafolla, Max Martínez and Jim Cody provided invaluable inspiration. As did my friend Juan Rodríguez. Thanks also to those who published my poems in periodicals and anthologies.

Reyes Cárdenas

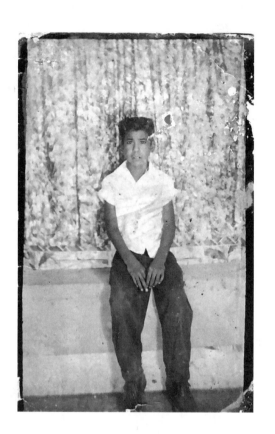

CONTENTS

POEMS FROM CHICANOPOET.BLOGSPOT.COM *221*
(2004-2010)

REYES CÁRDENAS: CHICANO POET

BY JUAN RODRÍGUEZ

The Chicano Movement, in its cultural nationalist stage (1965-1975), gave birth to a trinity of Tejano poets whose deep faith in the people (La Raza) of Aztlan was expressed in a personal gentleness of spirit[1] that countermanded the explosiveness and bravado of most Chicano poets of the time. Two of these poets, Jesús "Flaco" Maldonado[2] and Cecilio García-Camarillo,[3] left their native Tejas: Flaco to the Pacific Northwest, and Cecilio, in the years before his untimely death, to New Mexico. Only Reyes Cárdenas has remained close to his hometown of Seguín, "except for the year that I lost my way on the freeway and wound up in Lincoln, Nebraska."[4] And only Reyes has continually written from those hefty days (daze) of the Chicano Movement to the present, a life's work, much of which you can now enjoy in this ground-breaking, monumental collection:[5] *Reyes Cárdenas: Chicano Poet 1970-2010*.

Organized mostly in chronological order, this book is a 40-year retrospective of Reyes Cárdenas' life and work written from 1970-2010. It is divided into the following 11 sections with original black and white title-page illustrations for each section by L.A. David: Selections from *Chicano Territory* (1970); *Los Pachucos y La Flying Saucer* (1975, the only novella in this anthology, originally published in *Caracol* magazine); Selections from *Anti-Bicicleta Haiku* (1976); Selections from *Survivors of the Chicano Titanic* (1981); *Elegy for John Lennon* (1982); Selections from *I Was Never a Militant Chicano* (1986); *Homage to Robinson* (2008); *The Collected Poems of Artemio Sánchez* (2009); *Meeting Mr. Incognito* (2010); *Poems from chicanopoet.blogspot.com* (2004-2010); and *From Aztlan to the Moons of Mars: A Chicano Verse Novela* (2010). Of the eleven sections, five are selections from previous publications,[6] and six are new, never before published collections of poetry.

In *Chicano Territory* (1971, Caracol), his first book, Reyes affirms the tenets of the Chicano Movement: carnalismo (brother and sisterhood) and the union of the oppressed, while situating himself and his poetry in that whirlwind of social change. In fact, it is in the union of self and social situation that Reyes finds his reason for being both a Chicano and a poet. This explains why almost all of his poetry is rooted in the historical moment, and in his quest for personal meaning within that moment. In the title poem, for example, Reyes writes his version of an ars poética in which he presents himself as the humble, modest, humorous, calm, reclusive individual that he is:

> If you come by you'll see me in the back writing about
> Chicano territory.
> Out of my life have gone all the nagging doubts.
> And with them even my vieja.
> But I keep on writing as if nothing has happened.
> Sounds and colors drift into the poem
> and go out of it.
> This is what peace is all about.
> And when this poem passes by
> no one has to move out of the way.

In "For Tigre,"[7] Reyes, after listing some of the many injustices against Chicanos, ties the success of the Chicano Movement to poetry, which to him is the palpable representation of peace and justice. He writes: "But Aztlan won't die/Not with Chicanos and Chicanas fighting side by side,/fighting day and night until there's/nothing left but poetry." "I have found my place in life," he writes in the poem "PV," "It's not chasing carnalas, or throwing firebombs/but writing for La Causa/.../A carnala squats to piss/ in an alley after cerveza/It's amazing how free she is./And I have finally found my place in life,/even when I'm not writing."

Long before A.C. Weisbecker published his stereotypical *Cosmic Banditos: A Contrabandista's Quest for the Meaning of Life* (1986), and before Rosaura Sánchez' and Beatrice Pita's more engaging and Raza-correct *Lunar Braceros: 2025-2148* (2009), Reyes Cárdenas had ventured into the realm of science fiction with his farcical *Los Pachucos y La Flying Saucer* (1975), the first Chicano writer to do so, to my knowledge. While at first glance this may seem as if Reyes is stepping back from the social context of the 1970s to enter a purely imaginative world, it is not so, for his farce is a science fiction mini-version of Corky Gonzales' *I am Joaquín*,[8] insofar as it ties the pachucos—in a hilarious time collapse—to the Alamo, Davy Crockett, and Pancho Villa. His is an epic, culturally-steeped parody of Corky's work. It is as if Reyes writes the farce as a way to experience the freedom of writing about anything he wishes, while still anchoring himself in the Chicano world. In this way, he reaches universality of form, while keeping the specificity of Chicano reference in his work. To this freedom and specificity of reference, he returns with a more developed text in *From Aztlan to the Moons of Mars: A Chicano Verse Novela*, the last work included in this volume.

In *Anti-Bicicleta Haiku* (1976, Caracol), Reyes makes another attempt at exploring new forms for Chicano poetry. . .while having a good laugh. Inspired by two great Chilean poets, Nicanor Parra[9] and Vicente Huidobro,[10] Reyes parodies, to the point of mockery, a classical form, the haiku, in a conversationalist style, while leaving us to wonder what he is against: bicycles, really? Much like Huidobro, Reyes brings together words that are not easily associated in our ordinary world. Beyond this, and here the Chicano specificity, Reyes seems to be having some good-natured fun with alurista[11] and his way of writing.[12] For example, in "Los Aztecas Nomás No," Reyes mimics alurista's *Floricanto en Aztlán* (1971)[13] in form and content:

You don't want me   CILANTRO
in your brazos   TRIPAS DE COYOTE
like cooking
for me.
Longer poems
salen del miedo

Mi corazón
round cuando your face is fighting me.

BOCA . . .
que habla   TABLA

And at the end
of a ramita
a blossom
se cae
como tú.

It is not surprising that Reyes should be attracted to Vicente
Huidobro's belief in the poet's complete freedom to create a new
reality with words, an act that he called "creacionismo." So it
is fitting that Reyes makes Huidobro one of the *Survivors of the
Chicano Titanic* (1981, Place of Herons Press), one who takes Reyes'
advice: "If you lie/still, and breathe/calmly, you'll/ float inside
yourself" and save yourself from the sinking of "progress," and
heed the "Intimidations" that "...no one seems to notice./No one
is shocked/a foot away." Like Amilcar Cabral[14] advises, Reyes
is urging Chicanos to return to the source, the cultural source
from which we have been intimidated. We must return until, as
survivors, we develop "that glint in their eyes./That swaggered/
humility."

A more "creationist" poem is "Carmen,"[15] whose "...freckles
twirl away from your/shoulders like the universe./I mean, they
spin/a cocoon for a lozenge." A record of a day together, a day
of incongruities ("vagina, laundromat, coup d'etat"), "Carmen"
has the two poets find peace, "Like being stuck to the wall/of
injustice,/demure of poetic license,/peace nevertheless enters."
And in the end, the two forge congruity out of incongruity: "Later,
in your apartment/I see your face/ink-stained from writing so
much." Their real carnalismo is found in their lives as poets.

"Frugality on Sixth Street" and "Elegy for Joe Campos Torres" recall those who did not survive the Chicano Titanic: Max Martínez;[16] Santos Rodríguez, a twelve-year-old Chicano kid murdered in cold blood on July 24, 1973, by Dallas police officer Darrell Cain; and Joe Campos Torres, murdered by six Houston police officers in May of 1977. These deaths, the last two in particular, have caused "a pain that we/try to put in the trash," but find that "There's really/no place for this pain,/it doesn't even/belong here." ("Elegy for Joe Campos Torres").

After the presentation of the horrid violence and profound exasperation expressed in the poems referenced above, Reyes presents a beautiful meditation on death, and what remains of life after death. In "The Dragonfly,"[17] the delicate wings that "... could/have beat back any enemy". . ."failed in a critical instant." With the dragonfly in hand, "a mass of dryness" now, the poet "...regard[s] it and wash[es] away/the present for a moment" and thinks "... of the countless zig-zags, turns, and dives,/and stare[s] at the everlasting in its face." (Brackets, mine).

In the third section of *Survivors of the Chicano Titanic*, Reyes does something which he had rarely done up to that point in his writing career and has not done since, to my knowledge: he writes eight poems completely in Spanish. It's a tribute, I believe, to the Central American guerrillas who took the brunt of the dirty proxy wars that two Ronald Reagan administrations let loose on those small republics, particularly Guatemala, El Salvador, and Nicaragua. Out of the eight poems, "Poema Sandino,"[18] included in this collection, is arguably the best.

In what is perhaps his most accomplished, cohesive work, *Elegy for John Lennon*, Reyes turns from Latin American poetic influences to American popular culture, poetry and music specifically, as the source of his inspiration. And again, as a poet of peace, justice, and freedom, and as a double-subject Mexican-American, it is not surprising that he should write a paean to John Lennon, the British singer who gave the American Vietnam War protests its anthem, "Give Peace a Chance." Reyes combines references to American poets (Delmore Schwartz, John Berryman, Sylvia Plath, etc.) and singers (Buddy Holly, Michael Jackson, The Moonglows, etc.) as a way to situate Chicano culture in the greater cultural reality of the United States.

But as a social chronicler, as a poet who sticks close to home and to what is occurring around him in the immediate, Reyes extracts personal and social meaning from the cultural forces at work in the greater world. In "Casablanca," he writes: "I wear my hair like a charro/knowledge crunching from news/of the world, my white shirt/spiraling like words on the page/The cliff of my hometown is poetry/to the hunter and the hunted." In the end, however, "Stars glitter and evaporate [John Lennon, Buddy Holly, Michael Jackson]/while Atlas holds Texas over his head—/this rarefied air makes rednecks of us all." And it does so because "Mandela is a free man after 27 years,/but of course after 27 years in prison/nobody is a free man./And after forty-two years of American freedom,/I am not free, you are not free,/we are not free." And this is why "A few years later, while reclining/in the Oval Office,/Nixon would tell his aides, 'Fuck/the Constitution!' and eventually/ Ford pardoned the fornication—/but the Magical Mystery Tour/ Stops only in Paradise" ("The Magical Mystery Tour"[19]). The clash of fantasy with reality leaves the poet "to hallucinate an imaginary world/in which peace and justice/actually existed." (Brackets, mine).

In *I Was Never a Militant Chicano*[20] (1986), Reyes returns to the world he occupies, the Chicano reality of social oppression and of his personal dreams for peace, freedom, and justice, which are thwarted once again because "I was never/a militant Chicano/ but only because/I've always wanted/more than a revolution can provide." ("I Was Never a Militant Chicano"). And yet, he recognizes that something must be done to overturn the Chicanos' social situation, even if each solution to the problem is inadequate. He writes: "There's only one way/to go about it/so why put it off/ any longer?" ("If We Praise the Aztecs"). Ultimately, he concludes, the revolution begins with humanizing the self and others:

But today I am thirty-eight,
I gnaw at time;
and if by chance
a little injustice
crumbles somewhere
on Earth today,
then I celebrate.
If somewhere on Earth
someone becomes more human today,
then I celebrate.
And if it's me
who becomes more human,
then I celebrate
even more.

"The Poet's Birthday"

Homage to Robinson[21] is an anti-epic of sorts, a complete tale of an anti-hero, an antogonist who brings destruction to the world. The long poem represents Reyes' entry into the surreal world of a bourgeois, dehumanized protagonist, Robinson, who lives by his egotistical "conquistador instinct," especially as it comes to sex. But even here, in what should be the realm of feelings, the world of violence prevails. Mrs. Morse, Robinson's lover, finds that "Earlier on the way to Robinson's gray apartment/her heart beat like a cop's nightstick/against a skull." ("House of Robinson"). Robinson is incapable of feeling anything truly human, "When other people talked of joy or happiness/Robinson looked away/and banished such foolishness." ("The Sound of Ice Cubes"). Robinson is "a pterodactyl" that views the world "with pterodactyl eyes." (The Missing Links"). His serpent eyes and vision of the world are the reason Robinson avoids mirrors, "he partook of La Malinche/ because that's what white men do/he thought as he looked into the mirror to shave,/being careful not to make eye contact,/being careful not to look into his soul by accident." ("The Conquering Hero"). Reyes turns the Weldon Kees character into the empty white bourgeois man who lacks a soul.

In Robinson's world of non-feeling and immediate satisfaction, only the workers, the common folk who must forge a living in an objectified world, are real, endowed with feelings in a cold world of things that only exist for the use and pleasure of the bourgeois, of Robinson. In "King Kong" Reyes writes:

> The carpet gathers itself on the floor
> woven by machines
> sweated over by the working class,
> the metal frame of the bed
> put together in a dirty shop
> by the rough, callused hands
>
> which don't pick up the *New York Times*
> or use the *Tribune*
> only to patch a broken windowpane.
>
> The cannery workers
> who put the canned food in his pantry
> would ignore poetry unless it gave them a raise.

But in the end, it's Robinson's naked vision that prevails. When the city is left bare and barren, naked, and turned inside out, "Robinson nods goodbye to his friends,/walks down the street/ towards the cemented sky forever." ("The Naked City").

From the cold steel world of Robinson, Reyes moves to his hometown of Seguín, Texas and his past life there. But he returns as his alter-ego, Artemio Sánchez. *The Collected Poems of Artemio Sánchez* is a memoir full of playfulness and warmth delivered in typical Reyes humor. For example, Artemio is not Quetzalcoatl, the plumed-serpent, at the beach, instead he becomes "Artemio, The Toweled-Serpent" who "has lost the whole of Aztlan." What he has found in his return to the past is his calling, "The modern day Artemio/tries to use his poetry/as his hatchet/to carry out his hatchet jobs." ("Namesake").

Self-deprecation is the name of the game for Reyes:

> At the conference, Artemio tries to explain
> how he, as a poet, got to this point
> in his creative career.
>
> He goes back to his roots,
> the Olmec head of his great-grandfather,
> a lowly go-fer no doubt.
> And how Artemio groveled his way up
> from nothing in the white man's eyes,
> to nothing in his own brown community.
>
> "So it is this art I am obligated to ..."
> he curses and smiles.
> "It's our humor that brings us tears," he promises.
>
> "Flying Mexicana"

He is hilarious. In "The Hunt" he writes: "In a rush to impregnate every female,/we get trapped by the pleasure/that simmers at the hand." In "Flea Flicker" he has a good laugh at the expense of the white, heavy-set football players at Seguin High when they discover that the brown weakling writes poems for the school paper: "A dumb, puzzled look/on their stupid faces, thinking/ stinking Mexican sure has a way with words!" Finally, "if Artemio had any sense of identity,/it lay within, and without—/sole surviving son of la pinche Malinche." ("Identity Theft").

I suppose that it's every poet's dream to live in an imaginary, literary world where contact with famous poets and writers is ordinary and everyday, where the world of poetry and its inhabitants occupy the mind and body of the characters. It's a bourgeois world, for sure. Such is the world the poet's persona enjoys in *Meeting Mr. Incognito.*[22] It's a world of petty jealousies, rumors, light snobbery, frustrated sexual desires, faux intrigue where everyone "in the know" feels superior to those they consider to be less talented. Mr. Incognito, for example, turns out to be, according to the poet's persona, ". . .a goddamn Soviet poet,/he talks about oppression/ as if it was something bad,/he makes Siberia seem so cold." ("Meeting Mr. Incognito"). Because Mr. Incognito is drawing female admirers, the poet's persona is incensed. "Mr. Incognito is a proud and boastful/son of a bitch, all them Russians are,/but you and the rest of his groupies/cannot see that he's a pathological dictator." ("Coffee Klatch").

Despite the bourgeois flash, there's little in this world of art and artists, Reyes suggests. In the end, it's a vacuous world. In "Twenty Love Poems and a Cartoon" we read: "I see you are reading Neruda/as I climb into bed and wrest the remote/away from you. 'Hey, hey,' you tell me./'But you are reading that stupid book.' I look at you in amazement." Though the poet's persona loses the argument, later on that night he falls asleep watching a Bugs Bunny cartoon. Ultimately, what the poet's persona lives in the world of art, is as much a sham as "Mr. Incognito's Americanized Gobbledygook."[23]

After an 18-year publication gap,[24] Reyes enters cyberspace by posting hundreds of poems on his blog, chicanopoet.blogspot. com. With this move he finds the perfect couplet of message and media. The immediacy of the internet matches perfectly with what Reyes has done all of his writing career: write poetry "in place and in time," commenting on and at the moment. This allows him to display the full range of his work: situating the serious next to the humorous; the tragic next to the magic; the contemplative next to the quixotic; the autobiographical next to the ethnographic; the smirk next to the smile; and the present next to the past.

For those of us who have been on the Chiclit[25] train since it left the station in the 1960s, *Poems from chicanopoet.blogspot.com* is a special treat for its references to Chicano/a writers and poets, both living and dead. But I'll let you, the reader, enjoy this gem on your own. I promise you won't be the same after its read.

In *From Aztlan to the Moons of Mars: A Chicano Verse Novela*, the last section of this anthology, Reyes returns to the science fiction world he first entered in *Los Pachucos y La Flying Saucer*. As a result of "the racism/which was running rampant on Earth" ("The New Martians"), particularly these days in Arizona,[26] Chicanos have been "edicted" to the realms of outer space: the moon, Mars, the moons of Jupiter. "Of course he missed his wife/and kids back in Texas/but with so few jobs/back on earth/for a man his color/ since the new edicts/became the law of the land/space had become his only option." ("The Final Frontier Indeed, Piporro").

The odd and most humorous thing about the Chicano New Martians is that, in speech and culture, they are the same barrio Chicanos we would recognize today. The only difference is that in this brave new world, Chicanos are in control. And as such, they are masters of their actions, which gives them the opportunity for revenge, ("... Moctezuma's Revenge/No shit!") ("Cheech and Chong's Nice Dreams"), against their former rulers on Earth. All this happens when Isidra stumbles upon and opens a 100-thousand-year-old sarcophagus in which an ancient and powerful Mayan woman is found and awakened. She immediately kills some Chicanos before she returns to the sarcophagus. What to do with such a destructive power? Send it to Earth, of course! When the New Martians accomplish their revenge, wiping out all of the "whitey" Earthlings, they celebrate, and then: "The Mexicans/were again/ strangers in a strange land/alone in the universe . . ./For now." ("Brave New Chante").

And indeed, when Reyes wrote this last line to his final collection in this book, he surely must have felt as if he was living "alone in the universe," for after more than forty years of writing for and about his Chicano community, his work — up to now — has known little circulation and even less critical attention.[27] As he writes in the poem "I Was Never a Militant Chicano," "I was never/Like Raul Salinas,/alurista or Ricardo Sánchez," although he, like them, was "creating a new/world of poetry/out of a white wasteland."

But as he notes in the same poem, ". . . followers want/justice and liberty/and fairness, too." And while "I could never/shout like Tigre./But inside/(right here)/I guess I can/roar just as loud."

When I think of Reyes Cárdenas and his place in Chicano letters, my mind immediately places him alongside another great, but little known, Chicano artist, folk singer Sixto "Sugar Man" Rodríguez.[28] Despite the keen mastery of their respective art forms, both have been neglected — up to now — by the general American public and, sadly, by their own ethnic community. This may be because both are humble human beings who, unlike many of their colleagues, do not self-promote, preferring instead to let their art speak for itself. And in both cases, their art speaks in a thunderous voice that demands our attention.

My hope is that this ground-breaking book will be the means by which Reyes Cárdenas will indeed "roar" as loudly as any great poet of the past and present.

Juan Rodríguez, a Tejano, university professor and cultural critic, has written on Chicano Literature since its genesis in the late sixties. He has taught at various universities throughout the U.S. and for the last thirty years has worked at Texas Lutheran University in Seguín where he is currently an Associate Professor of English and the Director of Mexican-American Studies.

FOOTNOTES

1. I do not want to leave the impression that their poetry was/is gentle, it was not. What I mean is that their personal mode of being was/is characterized by a generosity of spirit toward humanity.

2. Jesús has published two books: *Sal y pimiento y amor* (1976), and *In the Still of My Heart* (1993).

3. Cecilio, as a poet, fiction writer, journalist, editor, publisher, and screenwriter, published more than seventeen chapbooks and *Caracol* magazine for many years.

4. From a private conversation between Reyes and myself.

5. To my knowledge, this is a first in Chicano letters. At almost 400 pages, and covering a 40-year period of the poet's life, it exhibits a representative selection of Reyes' previously published works, and brings to print in book form for the very first time, six new collections of poetry.

6. According to the editors, they selected works for this publication from the four previous books in which Reyes was the sole author, plus, *Los Pachucos y La Flying Saucer*. However, Reyes was also published in a fifth book, *Get Your Tortillas Together* (1976, Caracol), that was co-authored by Carmen Tafolla and Cecilio García-Camarillo. Below are a couple of his poems from that fifth publication:

Coyote Mind

I am trying to
talk
maybe even using
Indian sign language.

Ages ago the
brush on fire.

But the only fuel
there was
the coyote mind
working perfectly.

Now the
moon is wiped out.
A moonbeam aslant.

The Capote road
becomes a dark purple.
And the center of a
branch
pulls us together.

La Tracalada

La tracalada goes on
pero nada changes
the old things

the way tierrita
clings to piedras...
the way humo
leaves the fires...

the way that water
siempre sabe
como bajar...

the roots
will always know
how deep to go
sin tener que preguntar,
without having
to think twice.

7. Raymundo "Tigre" Pérez, from a group of early Chicano Movement poets who I named the "poetas retóricos" for their often bombastic, confrontational poetry, and who Reyes greatly admired for writing in a manner, tone, and style he could not practice in good faith.

8. "I am Joaquín," an epic poem that chronicles the history of Mexican-Americans, was the first text in Chicano history that most of us encountered in our lives.

9. Chilean poet whose *Poemas y anti-poemas* (1954) upset literary conventions in Latin American letters for its iconoclastic stance and for its debunking of classical literary forms.

10. Chilean poet whose epic "Altazor" is an example of his "creacionismo," the attempt to disconnect poetry from the external world, to produce a singular world made up of words that are as real as the objects in the world.

11. The prolific Chicano cultural nationalist poet of the sixties and seventies who popularized the concept of Aztlan among Chicanos, and who was also greatly influenced by the vanguardista poets of Latin America like Huidobro and Parra.

12. Throughout much of Reyes' poetry the reader will find cross-references, usually in a humorous manner, to his contemporary Chicano poets: alurista (as the aluristo phone in *From Aztlan to the Moons of Mars*), Carmen Tafolla, Ricardo Sánchez, Raul Salinas, Rebecca Gonzales, etc.

13. alurista's "Moongloom Dreams" will give the reader a sense of what I mean:

> pendiente cabellera
> roja luna
> mujer
>   I pity the fool
> standing

when you fly
meet the sun (in tears)
he knows not
  —your children dream
moongloom
  on their shoulders locks
rizos negros
  ilusión, morena
luna llena
  —de libertad
hair flowing—night
  —to see the sun

en la pirámide
  —hacia el sol,
volar
  —libres (I pity the fool!)

14. Amilcar Cabral was the outstanding intellectual and
revolutionary who liberated Guinea and the Cape Verde Islands
from the Portuguese, and who, because of that, Portuguese agents
killed in 1973. As part of the revolutionary act, the oppressed must
return to their cultural source, must stop aspiring to be like the
colonizer, he advocated.

15. Carmen Tafolla is a prolific poet, author, educator, and Reyes'
good friend and co-conspirator who is the City of San Antonio's
first Poet Laureate.

16. Chicano novelist, now deceased, author of *The Adventures of the
Chicano Kid and Other Stories* (1982, Arte Público Press), and one of
Reyes' closest friends in the Chicano literary world.

17. Thanks to a Reyes' e-mail dated January 3, 2013, I know that
this poem is inspired by César Vallejo's "The Spider" from his
most famous book *Los heraldos negros*. As a Modernist, Vallejo
sought freedom of expression in his work, free of previous forms
of writing poetry. In this belief, he and Reyes concur.

18.   **Sandino Poem** (English translation by Carmen Tafolla)

these things that drag us across the floor
we have to stand them up like a dried-up Christmas tree
we have to sprinkle water on them until they sprout leaves
until we can speak again
until we can move the century
the dresser that won't let us open the door
the torn sofa we cover with sheets

this cold that has us shivering day and night
this hail that comes in through the roof
this monied sun that burns our heads
we have to leave the house
to then be able to live in it freely

2.

these people that don't hear what's happening in the world
and even if they hear, they don't care, don't feel
don't understand that the world reaches us all

but we, we have to resist time
lift the pen, although it be with our bones
we have to offend those who close their eyes
so that even empty pages drown their sweet dreams
and they wake up coughing searching for air.

19. The name of a Beatles musical album and movie in which the characters had unspecified (mystery) magical adventures (tour).

20. In the interest of full disclosure, I will note that my and my ex-wife's publishing company, Relámpago Press Books, published this book.

21. Thanks to Reyes' e-mail of January 5, 2013, I learn that this homage is to the tragic American poet Weldon Kees' neurotic alter ego, Robinson, as can be seen in the following Kees poem:

Aspects of Robinson

Robinson at cards at the Algonquin; a thin
Blue light comes down once more outside the blinds.
Gray men in overcoats are ghosts blown past the door.
The taxis streak the avenues with yellow, orange, and red.
This is Grand Central, Mr. Robinson.
Robinson on a roof above the Heights; the boats
Mourn like the lost. Water is slate, far down.
Through sounds of ice cubes dropped in glass, an osteopath,
Dressed for the links, describes an old Intourist tour.
—Here's where old Gibbons jumped from, Robinson.

Robinson walking in the Park, admiring the elephant.
Robinson buying the Tribune, Robinson buying the Times.
Robinson saying, "Hello. Yes, this is Robinson. Sunday
At five? I'd love to. Pretty well. And you?"
Robinson alone at Longchamps, staring at the wall.

Robinson afraid, drunk, sobbing Robinson
In bed with a Mrs. Morse. Robinson at home;
Decisions: Toynbee or luminol? Where the sun
Shines, Robinson in flowered trunks, eyes toward
The breakers. Where the night ends, Robinson in East
Side bars.

Robinson in Glen plaid jacket, Scotch-grain shoes,
Black four-in-hand and oxford button-down,
The jeweled and silent watch that winds itself, the brief-
Case, covert topcoat, clothes for spring, all covering
His sad and usual heart, dry as a winter leaf.

Weldon Kees, from *The Collected Poems of Weldon Kees*, edited by
Donald Justice, University of Nebraska, 2003.

22. Although the worlds presented are at opposite poles, the title
recalls the alternative hip-hop song by the group A Tribe Called
Quest, especially the ending of that song:

But your mind can't contain Incognito's on the brain
So you chill by yourself don't really sweat nobody
Speak to all the brothers and say peace to every hottie
But lurkin in the ghetto is a germ that insists
Should you back the germ away or utilize your fists
Neither of the two, just continue with your thoughts
And rush away your pain with the power of the thought
Ain't got no time for girls, cause girls be on some bull
Checkin for a nigga who got crazy pull
On some deep rooted sexual, highly intellectual
Not checkin for the fame although it's perpetual
I enter the world the same way I'll exit
If you really think the groove,
Then hey glad you checked it
Cause Incognito's strong not urkin like a blister
Before you speak about me, make sure you call me Mister.

23. In my opinion, an apt description of A Tribe Called Quest's lyrics.

24. Reyes notes that he did write during this period, but that the notebooks have been lost or misplaced.

25. Not to be confused with Chicklit (an English and American literature subgenre), or Chicalit, Chicklit's Chicana equivalent. Chiclit is my word for Chicano literature in general.

26. This fact does not escape Reyes: "Yes, a large number of New Martians/are descendants of the Arizona Mexicans/who were rounded up and sent to the/penal colony that once made up Mars." ("Down Under"). See also his poem "Dogs Are Shakespearean, Children are Strangers in a Strange Land."

27. This is Reyes' first book publication in 27 years.

28. For a great appreciation of this artist's life and talent, see the 2012 documentary film *Searching for Sugar Man*.

FOR NANCY

Selections from

CHICANO TERRITORY

1970

CURANDERO

For Julián Cárdenas

The carnales and carnalas
at the Chicano Moratorium.
Running as fast as they can
they still can't outrun the mace.
Elsewhere, two Chicanas have made it.
They cower near a building.
Everybody's running for their lives.
Three Brown Berets are clubbed.
The whole world is in shambles.
Only another Indian takeover
can start things going the other way.
And if Reies is out of prison,
he will know what to do,
swooping out of the mountains, again.

LA LLORONA

Two FBI agents executed on the Pine Ridge Reservation
the Indian Wars are not over yet!
The carnales still have to fight.
Russell Means and Dennis Banks
fly backwards over a pony.
And land in the middle of the Chicano Movement.
That's where they belong,
and we belong with them.
The word indio means us, too.
And the word Chicano means them.
And this is not a pun on Russell's name.
It's a dangerous life we live…
But a life filled with azure, oblong skies
and beautiful cumbersome canyons, wide plains,
barrio children, Sioux mothers, and la llorona finally happy.

CHICANO TERRITORY

My long black and white hair attracts too much attention.
Especially in a little redneck town like Seguin,
but even walking around inside a peach tree
I attract too much attention.
I guess you have to feel like a poet
to write a poem.
I don't live in a shack on Fourth Street for nothing!
If you come by you'll see me in the back writing about
Chicano territory.
Out of my life have gone all the nagging doubts.
And with them even my vieja.
But I keep on writing as if nothing has happened.
Sounds and colors drift into the poem
and go out of it.
This is what peace is all about.
And when this poem passes by
no one has to move out of the way.

FOR TIGRE

And Tigre's always talking about death.
There's no need to ask why, or how…
just ask Santos!
There's too much death in Aztlan,
too many carnales shot down in the streets
because they won't surrender.
Shot down because they don't want to be slaves anymore.
Shot down because they want to unionize…
because they strike…because they picket…
Carnales shot down because they tell the truth.
Children killed by pigs…
But Aztlan won't die!
Not with Chicanos and Chicanas fighting side by side,
fighting day and night until there's
nothing left but poetry.

MANIFESTO

Sure, now it doesn't matter.
Outside there's a Chicano
flying upside down.
Across the street
someone calls this a barrio,
and then goes into the next line.
Try to catch a gringa by the tail
you can't.
Her pink buttocks on Padre Island.
Gringos adore square poetry.
They're in Mexico chasing Villa,
leave them there.
Here in the Juan Seguín Manifesto
a pachuco scurries.
Stop that punk he's crazy.
The democrats love the Buddha.
An Italian painting falls off the wall,
that's what I was going to tell you.

WOMEN

Prieta, realizing that I don't want you, realizing that
I don't love you anymore, it's like you
slapping me for touching you abajo.
Hell, love is funnier than Cantinflas...
Perhaps it's because meeting a woman like Dora
I see that I need to be free from the past.
Free from being in love with a high school girl,
or the woman you are now,
beautiful, but distant.
Sure, I can't deny that without you
I wouldn't be a poet, or whatever it is
that I am.
And you Dora, even if you don't love me,
thank you too, for your tenderness, for
your Chicanismo, for being so special,
and thank you Janay for so long ago,
everything, your bare shoulders in
Bruce's Volkswagen bus...

PV

I have found my place in life.
It's not chasing carnalas, or throwing firebombs,
but writing for La Causa.
And then of course I change my mind,
to fall madly in love over the edge,
but I'm a coyote.
Sly as an underside of tortillas.
No one can really halt the Movimiento.
It's no runaway stagecoach in the movies.
Smart enough not to perish.
I haven't worn khaki in so long
or filled a guitar with rain.
Or here is a similar image:
A carnala squats to piss
in an alley after cerveza.
It's amazing how free she is.
And I have finally found my place in life,
even when I'm not writing.

CHAPTER ONE

It was a few nights ago it started happening. I said to Nacho, "Hey, man, what's going on, you see that light, and the noise, man, what is it?" For a while Nacho couldn't move, he froze like if he was somewhere in Greenland. Finally, he blurted out, "It sure as hell ain't La Llorona."

Anyway, it was a Saturday night when me and Nacho ran into La Flying Saucer. Man, we were scared, we thought: Hell, those gringos were right about the Martians.

But you ask why we call her "La" instead of "El," well, it's because it turned out to be a female flying saucer.

We didn't want to tell anyone because we were afraid they'd call us locos or pendejos. You know other pachucos, man, they'd call you joto, a queer, if you went around saying you'd seen a flying saucer. Naw, man, so we didn't tell anyone.

"Le damos en la madre, yo le doy patadas y tú le das cadenazos," Nacho said, after he recovered. So we rushed up to La Flying Saucer, man, we beat the hell out of it, le dimos una chinga.

As Nacho proceeded inflicting his deadly kicks with his pointed red shoes, I went around to the other side of La Flying Saucer. Man, that was the biggest surprise of my life. There were two breasts sticking out. That's how we found out it was a girl.

Nacho really got a kick from that (no punishment intended). Nacho decided to suck on one of the breasts to see if it was real. "Wow, it's really good, man, try the other."

I said, "What the fuck is wrong with you, I ain't going to suck on that flying saucer's tit, man, you're crazy!"

Suddenly La Flying Saucer shot some sort of ray that knocked Nacho on his back. Then a very feminine voice yelled, "What do you think I am, a whore?"

Nacho was so flabbergasted he began apologizing right away, "Perdóname señora, no sea así."

I whispered to Nacho, "Órale, ese, wátchate, this ruca, no telling what she's going to do to us," but it's hard to shut Nacho up.

I put my hand in my pocket and got a hold of my fila, my knife, just in case.

When La Flying Saucer quería saber que planeta she was on, man, we didn't hesitate.

"Dis is San Anto," I was so scared I didn't know whether it was me or Nacho talking.

Then she told us this story: Something had malfunctioned, and she had been forced to land here. It seems her food supply had been contaminated by the computer disorder. She said that we had to bring her food.

Nacho ran off to his house, and I went home, too, to raid the kitchen. I got some tortillas and cold frijoles and started back. Nacho was already there. He'd brought chile and menudo.

"What's wrong with you, Nacho?" I asked, "you'd better not give her that chile, she might get pissed off at us si le pica."

But before we could get rid of it, some laser pulled everything to what looked like a mouth. After an hour of silence she told us to go home and return next evening. "Tu bruja is my command," dijo Nacho.

Next morning la jefa was really enojada, "what happened to all the tortillas and beans? Have you been feeding that skinny Rosa of yours? ¡Le voy a decir a tu papá!" I said, "ya, jefa, agüítela."

Then she started the whole thing all over again. "And what are you doing up so early in the morning? It's not even noon yet."

Man, I just got up and left. Next thing you know she would have told me was to get a job, etc., etc.

Nacho y sus lagañas were awake already, too. "Were we dreaming last night?" he asked hopefully.

"I wish we had been dreaming."

"Yeah," I said, "but this afternoon I'm going to take Rosa to the park, it might be the last time I ever see her."

That night when Nacho and I got there: "Hey, Nacho, do those breasts still look good to you?" I was making a joke so as not to shake with fear.

We had been there but for a minute when she startled us. "Good, you are back. I need more food, I have been working hard trying to correct my computers, it will not be much longer. Go now."

"What are we gonna do, man?" Nacho shouted at me. "I can't go home to steal any more food, that menudo I ripped off was for today. My old man always has menudo on Sunday mornings."

"I don't know what we're going to do, why ask me? Túmbale feria a alguien, borrow some money."

Nacho eventually remembered that a cousin of his owed him

three dollars. Somehow we managed to get enough to buy six hamburgers for La Flying Saucer.

"This thing's eating better than us."

"Shut up, Nacho, I don't want to hear anything about it."

When we got there she told us to sit. She began to eat. It looked like she had enjoyed the Mexican food a lot better.

We'd brought an old battered up record player with us so as we waited for whatever was next, we listened to music. We were behaving as if this flying thing was an amiga.

We were completely unprepared for what happened next. First we thought La Flying Saucer had gone nuts.

Imagine our surprise when we saw Rosa near some bushes screaming her head off. Beside her was her best friend Leticia, and she was screaming even louder.

Me and Nacho rushed over. We finally calmed them down, but they had turned white as a gabacho. They couldn't move.

We told them the whole story. And to keep them from fainting, we persuaded them to dance. Their knees were shaking like ours. When La Flying Saucer spoke, Rosa and Leticia seemed a little scared, but were somewhat assured by the feminine voice. "What is this thing you do?" I answered, "We're bailando, you know, dancing?" Man, we couldn't help but be astounded by what occurred next. La Flying Saucer was trying to learn how to dance. "'Tá de aquellas, esa," Nacho said, having once again recovered his acid sense of humor, "órale, aviéntate esta polka."

And she tried that, too.

CHAPTER TWO

Well, man, La Flying Saucer danced so much that she collapsed. She was lying on her back, she looked very pale and just before she fainted she told us that it was going to rain. She said she hated rain, and that we must find her a place to stay.

Nacho turned to me and to the girls and said, "We sure can't take her home!"

It was already an hour afterwards and we hadn't figured out where to take her. Eventually Rosa came up with an idea that we take refuge at the Alamo. "¡'Tás tonta, Rosa, you're loca!" everybody yelled, but really that was the only place we could take her. We made a travois. It took mucho pulling but we got her there. The battle for the Alamo was in progress. Mexicans and gringos running all over the place. Nobody noticed us, so we rushed the front door. We ended up in a small room at the back. We lay down beside a wounded Texan. Dijo el vato he was James Bowie y el vato had una fila más grande than anything I'd ever seen.

"I'm a humble and a modest man, and I never brag, but I call this a Bowie knife," el gringo told us.

Nacho took it from him and started throwing it all over the place. Just about then La Flying Saucer woke up. Her brain must have still been a little hazy because she turned to Bowie and I guess she thought he was a flying saucer, too. She seemed to be talking in her native language. It puzzled the gringo.

Leticia related the whole story to Bowie. No sooner had she finished when Bowie sprang to his feet and tried to slit La Flying Saucer's throat. Gringos, you can't take them anywhere. We pulled him off of her. La Flying Saucer was about to take care of him herself.

You could hear gunfire and cannon blasts all around. La Flying Saucer and us ate. Finally, the aroma of the tortillas got to Bowie. He asked us for some.

Nacho and me had to go look for wood. It was getting dark and we wanted a fire. We gathered rifle butts for about five minutes. Gringos and Mexicans were dead side by side. When we got back, las rucas, Rosa y Leticia, had the record player going full blast. Rosa whispered to me to look at Bowie and La Flying Saucer. They were having a conversation como unos buenos amigos.

It rained that night. Next day the Mexicans wiped out the gringos. They broke into the room in which we were in and shot Bowie, and were about to shoot us, too, but La Flying Saucer's lasers made them immobile. Then a door opened on her left side. She said we must get in. Looking out through the window we could see the Alamo below us. The streets of San Antonio got smaller and smaller. Scanning the Southwest with her computers she decided that repairs could be better effected in an isolated area, but we must go along with her to gather food for her and to answer questions which she, as an alien on Earth, could not uncover no matter how intelligent she be. The isolated area turned out to be Los Ángeles. We spent a few weeks of calm.

La Flying Saucer let us wander through the barrio when she didn't have anything for us to do. We had learned a lot from her. Meanwhile, she too had been learning things from us. Rosa and Leticia had persuaded her to wear a blouse. She had three blouses now.

Well, just when todo estaba de aquellas, these stupid American sailors and soldiers started going through the barrio beating up pachucos and anybody else that got in their way. Sometimes there would be fights on every corner. We decided we'd get into it, too. La Flying Saucer said she wanted to go with us.

"¡No sabes ni tirar patadas!" Nacho laughed.

"Sé mejor que tú, pendejo." La Flying Saucer had learned Spanish.

The five of us headed down the street. There were about ten sailors on a streetcar. We rushed them. Kicking and punching we dragged them off. Man, La Flying Saucer had four of them on the ground. She was kicking the hell out of them. When a sailor got a hold of her hair, she lost her temper. There was a flashing light. Two or three blocks had been disintegrated. Y no les tengo que decir that the sailors were nowhere in sight.

By then we were bored of streetfighting so we went surfing. La Flying Saucer built sand castles. That afternoon we saw a Japanese submarine surface. The Japanese commander came out just long enough to drink salt water with chopsticks. La Flying Saucer was drunk, she had too much tequila. One minute she'd be flying crazily, the next minute she'd be snoring. Later that night she disappeared and she didn't return until breakfast. We were eating peanut butter and jellyfish. "¿Qué pasa, lagañosos?" she said, "I just got back from the Alamo. I went to look for Bowie's knife."

"Y no es todo," she had brought four horses for us. So that evening we rode down Main Street and beat up some more sailors. La Flying Saucer didn't feel like fighting, instead she stayed behind and devoured about two hundred dozen tamales. Afterwards she joined us at Malibu Beach. We didn't have much fun, man, the Army was after us. "Esa babosa de La Flying Saucer had to blow up half of Los Ángeles." Anyway, pretty soon tanks and jet bombers were all over us. We jumped into La Flying Saucer. She was yelling, "¡Vámonos!"

"What I need is a health spa," La Flying Saucer kept insisting.

Leticia knew of one in Tierra Amarilla, New Mexico.

We hadn't been there but a second when this vato named Reies López Tijerina came up to us and asked if we wanted to join his band of guerrillas.

"¡Órale, desgraciado, wátchate what you call me!" Nacho was infuriated.

"N'ombre, vato, you're not a gorilla, you're a chango," giggled Rosa.

The next day we took over the Tierra Amarilla Courthouse. La Flying Saucer took off her blouse and wore it as a headband. The strategy of the police was to starve us out. Unfortunately for them La Flying Saucer had repaired herself and now she could produce food and water. So we could, if we wanted, hold out forever. The girls kept the record player going day and night for the whole year we were there. La Flying Saucer decided to have some fun making the sheriff's clothes disappear. He started running around naked. Then she proceeded to do the same thing to the deputies. We couldn't stop laughing. Soon she had every gabacho in New Mexico running around naked. We watched the news on television. The Air Force didn't know what to do. And whenever the Army started to advance its tanks, La Flying Saucer would turn them into tortillas all over the place. Of course, after a year one gets tired of one place, so La Flying Saucer said it was time to leave. We said goodbye to Reies and the other Alianzistas and then zoomed off.

CHAPTER THREE

Only La Flying Saucer knew where we were going. Suddenly, we were flying through the stars. In unison all four of us started screaming, "¡hijodelachingada!" Nacho was raving, "¡Esta desgraciada, what the hell is wrong with this bitch, y la jefa is probably worried by now!"

"Shut up, Nacho," Rosa said, "your mother's lucky that you've disappeared, but that's more than I can say for us!" Yet, deep down inside we were certain that we would never see our families again. We had accepted that for more than a year already.

Then La Flying Saucer said, "No sean gallinas, don't be cowards, zbeqi nolgnnh, we're going to the world I come from, vamos pa' mi casa."

"What the hell does zbeqi nolgnnh mean?" asked Leticia , then quickly added, "never mind, I don't want to know."

There's really no way to describe her planet. No barrios, no Mexican food, etc. But she lived in a sort of city, a giant city whose buildings floated in the ground. "In the ground," it's weird, and you really can't imagine it until you see it with your own eyes. There were other flying saucers, all females, running, dashing about. La Flying Saucer looked out of place wearing her blouse, but none of the other flying saucers seemed to notice it.

It was a few days after we arrived that something crazy happened. La Flying Saucer had told us that we must say the word, or whatever it was, "rjenxa," each morning or the planet's gravity would pull our bodies apart. Anyway, we said, "chingatumadre" and didn't listen to her. Like I was saying, a few days later we woke up and found that our legs and arms were missing. They were stuck to the ceiling. We were horrified and started repeating "rjenxa, rjenxa, rjenxa." Almost immediately our limbs fell back in place. From then on we tried to be more careful.

Our food consisted of something even more fantastic. Servant flying saucers brought a box (something like a transistor radio) called a food transmitter. We had to listen to the sound it made. After we heard it, we felt full as if we had eaten thirty-five dozen enchiladas apiece.

Yet, however weird La Flying Saucer's planet was, we were free to do anything we wanted to do. Almost every afternoon we would go to what looked like a park. It was usually crowded with flying saucers. We would listen to music and dance. Occasionally, La Flying Saucer would come along and dance, too. And eventually the other flying saucers began to dance, first a little unsure, then really letting themselves go. Sometimes Rosa and Leticia would get jealous because we danced with the flying saucers.

"¿Por qué no hay hombres flying saucers?" Leticia blurted out angrily. And it was curious, there were no male flying saucers, or at least we hadn't seen any so far. One day we asked La Flying Saucer about it.

"Bueno, pues, this is the way it is, esos; I hadn't told you anything because I didn't think it mattered. Anyway, a long time ago my father also landed on Earth. It so happened that he became acquainted with a Mexican named Pancho Villa. They became amigos, each exchanging knowledge, and Villa decided to pretend to have himself assassinated. Then he came back to our planet with father. Incidentally, the name of our planet is Gogogirl. It is an ancient name meaning Planet of Breasts. So, after many years, Villa learned all there was to learn about our powers and secrets. He started gathering followers and organized a revolution. That's where our men are, they're fighting with Pancho Villa."

"But what is the revolution all about, what caused Villa to rebel?" I asked.

"Well, Villa es muy loco, he wants to change the whole food system of the planet. Him and his followers make and eat tortillas and frijoles."

"But why is it wrong?" asked Leticia. "You ate tortillas and beans while you were on Earth."

"Yes, but that was on Earth. Here on Gogogirl we are permitted to only sound. Of course there is nothing wrong with revolution; we welcome it. You yourselves may want to join Villa, and if you ever decide to, just let me know. I will take you there. Nobody ever dies because both sides have the same weapons…"

So that was that!

That afternoon me and Rosa realized that we wanted to get married. When we told this to Nacho and Leticia, they too decided to get married. A double wedding. La Flying Saucer said she'd arrange everything. She was happy. She told us that she would invite our fellow earthling Villa to the wedding.

So it was. Villa walked in magnificently to the building at which the ceremony was going to take place.

"Howdy, vatos, ¿cómo les va? ¿Quehúbole, muchachas? You are truly beautiful señoritas. Congratulations."

We became good camaradas. Pancho was the best man and afterwards at the dance, he danced and danced with La Flying Saucer all night. They looked at each other as though they were in love. When they went back to their table to sit, he kissed her quietly. And we left on our honeymoon.

In a few weeks we joined Villa's army. La Flying Saucer took us to Villa's camp. It was on the other side of Gogogirl. He gave us proton guns and we went out on patrol. La Flying Saucer hung around with us to teach us how to carry on a revolution. "You sure it's not because you want to be near Villa?" Rosa kept questioning her. But La Flying Saucer blushed and would not say anything. Standing on a hillside, we looked back down to the campsite and saw Villa playing a guitar. Nacho guessed that he was practicing so he could serenade La Flying Saucer that night.

CHAPTER FOUR

When we got back from patrol, Pancho did indeed serenade La Flying Saucer. Pancho tocaba la guitar de aquellas, but he couldn't sing worth a damn. Nacho started imitating Pancho's voice. It was almost a girlish voice. We could see Pancho and La Flying Saucer over in the shadows of some nearby air trees (these were as the name implies: made totally of air!). Anyway, los zonzos were kissing and hugging, y quien sabe que más estarían haciendo. La Flying Saucer had discarded her blouse earlier that evening. Finally, when they finished fooling around, Pancho gave us a progress report on the revolution. "N'ombre, carnales, everything's going great. Chingos de flying saucers are comin' over to our side. Creo que we're going to win this guerra within unos cuantos centuries. Bueno, es todo, I just want to conclude with our revolutionary slogan: 'Frijoles and tortillas para siempre, and no more sound food!'" Everybody threw their sombreros up in the air and some got stuck in the air trees. La Flying Saucer was at it again, drinking tequila.

"Ya no tomes, esa," Leticia scolded La Flying Saucer, "you know you can't drink."

"'Tás pendeja, Leticia," retorted La Flying Saucer. But she stopped drinking anyway because she knew Leticia was right.

Next morning we didn't wake up until early afternoon. Villa woke us up.

"¡Párense, huevones! ¡Ustedes también, huevonas!" Villa was still in his leather pajamas. Me and Rosa stumbled over to the jeep where La Flying Saucer was sitting sleepy-eyed. Villa was still trying to wake Nacho and Leticia.

"Where we going?" asked Rosa. La Flying Saucer muttered something unintelligible. So we climbed into the jeep and when Villa, Nacho and Leticia joined us, we took off. Villa looked grim now. We knew something was worrying him. He had to tell us what was on his mind.

"Carnales, carnales, I guess I was a little too optimistic last night, I mean, about the revolution. It looks like we're going to have to postpone it. Last night I got a letter from the President of Gogogirl…he wants us to join him in fighting invaders…"

I interrupted him, "What invaders?"

"Hold your caballos," he shouted. "The invaders are called Mariachis; they are a warlike race. They are ancestors of the mariachis on Earth, but these Mariachis are awful. They have been conquering worlds since the dawn of the universe. They are killers, they are horrible beasts."

Meanwhile, even La Flying Saucer had become scared. Obviously, she already knew of the Mariachis. Later on we found out she had only heard of them in history books. Mariachis had never come close to Gogogirl yet.

We kept on driving to the Capitol City. Flying saucers were streaming out of the city like in Japanese monster movies. The whole population was hysterical. Villa contacted his troops to converge with Gogogirl's Army.

"Dis is where we're going to make our stand," Villa whispered nervously.

For the next couple of days there were frantic meetings. But while the Army and civilian officials were running around, me and Nacho were getting our knives and chains ready. Rosa and Leticia took out our old record player. We danced.

"I wonder if these Mariachis cantan o no?" asked Rosa.

"Pues, I don't know," said Nacho, "but I'm sure as hell getting tired of these old records, tan todos rayados, y comoquiera, they remind me of all these stupid flying saucers."

Nacho was right. We were all tired of this planet. We longed to be back in San Anto filoreando otros vatos, going to the Alameda to see Cantinflas o Luis Aguilar. Las rucas también estaban agüitadas.

"¡Allí vienen, allí vienen!" gritó Villa. It scared the hell out of us. There were hundreds of spacecrafts approaching the city from the sky. The spacecrafts were camouflaged with bushes.

"¿Qué tienen esos babosos?" Nacho said. And everybody started screaming with laughter. Camouflaging their spacecrafts with bushes! We laughed so much our stomachs hurt.

They landed. We braced ourselves. Some of the spacecrafts must have had lousy pilots because they hit the ground so hard that the bushes fell off. We roared with laughter again; we couldn't stop our carcajadas.

It took awhile for the craft doors to open. Finally, we could hear someone's angry voice coming out of one of the crafts that had landed near us.

"¿Qué fregadas tienen? What kind of piloto eres, animal?" It must have been a general yelling at the pilot. Suddenly the Mariachis stumbled out. They were dressed just like the mariachis back home. They had their instruments ready to play.

All of us waited anxiously...we waited for them to charge. Then they started playing; they could not play anything; they were all untuned. Me and Nacho charged them. Then Villa, La Flying Saucer and everybody else followed us. Los pataliamos muy feo. Quedaron todos tirados. We thought it was all over when suddenly, out of the spacecrafts, herds of horses came running out. They too were dressed like Mariachis; they charged while playing "Adelita." This really upset Villa.

"¿Qué se traen, what the hell are you doing playing my song, la canción de mi revolución?"

So there we are, exhausted, but having to fight again. Y los caballos se avientan pa' las patadas. Nacho gets kicked in the balls. I hear him yell, "¡Pinche buey!" He gets up and goes on fighting.

The battle goes on for two days. We corral the last of the horses. Caballos mendigos. They gave us a tougher fight than the Mariachis. No wonder the Mariachis have been tearing the universe a new one.

CHAPTER FIVE

"That's one of the worst pleitos I've ever been in; esos caballos se avientan," said Nacho. He looked tired. Meanwhile, the prisoners were being led away.

"What will happen to them?" preguntó Leticia.

"Well, the Mariachis will stay here and learn our ways, or Pancho's way. It will be up to them. But the horses must go," answered La Flying Saucer.

"¿Por qué?" Rosa insisted.

"Obviously, tonta, they can't be taught to say 'rjenxa,' and you know what happens whenever you don't say 'rjenxa' each morning. We'd have pieces of horses floating all over the place. How would you like to keep running into colas de caballos every day?" La Flying Saucer had a point.

"But how will they be disposed of?" I asked.

Just at that moment Pancho drove up in his jeep. He had been at a meeting with Gogogirl officials. He told us that out of a total of two million Mariachis and caballos, there had been but one casualty. That unfortunate one was a mare; she had a miscarriage. On our side three flying saucers were wounded by thorns from the bushes which had camouflaged the invader's spacecrafts. But all were recuperating well. Also, about four thousand Mariachis were complaining of headaches. It was not yet known whether it was from playing their untuned instruments, or from landing so hard. Most of the Mariachis wore almost unrecognizable sombreros, probably from bouncing around inside those damn cucaracha spaceships.

Pancho said that since the crisis was over, we should go back into the mountains again.

"¿Mira lo que nos dieron, look what the Gogogirl government gave us," Pancho said excited, "in appreciation for our help?"

Pancho was pointing to a fleet of ten helicopters. But they were weird things. The seats were located on the propeller blades. Pancho climbed aboard, happy as a child. He turned it on and the seats and blades stood still, but the rest of the helicopter started going round and round. Soon Pancho was up in the air, circling overhead, really proud of himself. He picked us up and we went to our camp.

La Flying Saucer stayed behind, but a few days later she joined us.

"Aquí les traigo sus medals, vatos. Y a ustedes también, esas."

"But what for?" asked Rosa.

"For helping us defend our planet," La Flying Saucer said. She'd also brought a letter of thanks from the President. So we put on the medals. We had a party. La Flying Saucer had brought over six Mariachis that chose to join Villa's army. Pancho was happy; he showed them how to tune their instruments, and he taught them a few songs. Before the night was out, they were playing really good música. La Flying Saucer was drinking, but not too much. I went over and asked her about the caballos. "Well, ese, I don't know what we'll do with them. Esos caballos no se agüitan. We're having trouble with them. They've rebelled and taken over the prison."

I interrupted, "But how did they do it?"

"Well, we think they hit a guard on the head with a horseshoe."

"What will be done about it?" I asked.

"Nothing. We'll just wait until tomorrow when the 'rjenxa factor' will do the work for us."

Next morning we flew to the prison. It looked like a disaster area. We couldn't help but laugh, yet we felt sorry for the caballos. Flying saucers were all over the place trying to put the horses back together. We helped.

"Nacho, don't be so mean!" Leticia was shouting. Nacho was putting two tails on one horse, and sticking out his tongue at Leticia. I guess Nacho got a little careless and the caballo kicked him.

Pancho was sitting in his helicopter. He looked angry. He finally came up to us; he lost his cool, ya no se pudo controlar. He was addressing La Flying Saucer.

"¿Qué tienen los leaders de Gogogirl? Do they expect my army to help them put together these animals every day? We won't have time to continue the revolution. Why don't they get rid of them?"

We were beginning to realize why, although we didn't want to admit it to ourselves. Since the day of the invasion, the sky had changed color. It had turned from brown to blue. Atmospheric conditions had changed as the invader's spacecrafts went through the air. No one could fly out of the planet anymore. The scientists knew, but they didn't want to say anything because they knew it would cause a panic.

So the horses would have to stay. We must either teach them to talk, or get used to putting them together again each morning. After a few months of this, the ritual became known as PCT duty—Putting Caballos Together. The caballos gradually got used to it. It seemed like they even enjoyed it. We sort of got used to it ourselves, too. Eventually we found that if we didn't put on their tails, we finished a lot sooner. No more colas. So before long the caballos were tailless. ¡Que gacho! But the horses didn't mind.

Yet nobody seemed really concerned at being trapped. That is, nobody except us. We knew que if we were to get home, the "blue atmosphere" must be destroyed. Rosa wrote this poem called, "Perdidos En Otro Mundo":

We are stuck on Gogogirl,
can't go back to our own world!
Can't go back to the barrio,
can't hear KCOR!
Can't go to Brackenridge Park,
to court and spark!
We are far away from home
where outer space caballos roam.
And even La Flying Saucer
says there's no hope for nosotros.
While the sky remains blue
there's nothing to do.
Can't do anything but wait.
¡Ay, que fea fate!!!!!

SELECTIONS from

ANTI-BICICLETA HAIKU
1976

BEATRIZ CÁRDENAS ENOJADA

I'm reading
"Rin Tin Tin's patadas y orejas"
a toda madre
just for the hell of it.

Beatriz enojada
at me.
¿Por qué será?

Las ramas don't
obey a damn thing
like the second radiator
en este Studebaker quebrado.

Mi vida's going
and coming
hasta que
sí before dawn
like at Puente Prieto didn't vato loco.

AGUA JACKETS

Marxist leanings   ESOS
o lo que dejan   VATOS
los last
amores.
Muevo
mi pata inside
the Gulf of Mexico
con Asor.

Años pasan things change
las cositas
but terror.
Mickey Mouse, your cejas French…French…
become the tail
de una
yegua that's back again
volando…Vaseline.

And Italy crumbles
cuando tengo mucho.
Cuando tengo muchas palabras
that never decide like agua jackets.

POEMAS PARA AMIGOS

Poemas para amigos
enemigos
trigo growing
outside La Llorona bowlegged.

Sí, last time
que te, "Buscarte."
Saqué el tren, "Tamales Lagrimosos"
from its cabin.

Counter-clockwise
y counter-revolution
son la misma cosa
that suffices
una female crow.

Siguiéndole oblivion
Cecilio bending Laredo   TE DIJE
like if it
was algo.

LA CARA DE MI RUCA

No puedes sacar   NIÑOS CULEROS
your face Lloronita   MUERTOS, OK
del basement.

El Cucuy
was here
agarrándose del arroyo.

All of them
vatos y rucas hinder the arroyo.

But what can you
tell them
que no te
den chingazos.

KNUCKLES AL OJO
PATADAS AL GROIN

Anyway, Dios
no puede bailar
like your face.

LOS AZTECAS NOMÁS NO

You don't want me
in your brazos,
like cooking
for me.

CILANTRO
TRIPAS DE COYOTE

Longer poems
salen del miedo.
Mi corazón
round cuando your face is fighting me.

BOCA...
que habla
And at the end
of a ramita
a blossom
se cae
como tú.

TABLA

UN AYER DE INDIOS

Tus piernas
y mi cara go a long way
and come back
así son,   "Sonido."

Your legs
and truck
are wet,
calientitas.

OTRA TRUCK

If you walk para siempre
you'll always find
something warm
algo pendejo.

BRAZOS CUATRO
BRAZOS CUATRO
BRAZOS CUATRO
BRAZOS CUATRO

THE DALLAS NUMERO UNO
MEANINGFUL PICO DE ESTRELLA

En otro poema
I've used
vato as the verb bonito.

Patada
dancing, reliving
Denver bombas
nos dan en la madre de aquellas!

SPIDER ARAÑA
your lips
crossing
el arroyo seco…THERE GOES CHUY.

Simple mundo, COSQUILLAS EN INDONESIA
de ramas.
Crystal City Kitty.

There's a hole, vato,   Anti-Bicicleta Haiku
un pozo outside.
Santos trece años
went through it tontito.

POEMA AL PUENTE PRIETO

LA VIDA begins
un largo beso
de Coyote Man.

                    La Virgie's
                    adaptability

Saco
"RADIOS, 1931"
or las llantas coloradas
de forgotten
hormigas.   AMIGAS.

Muevo…MUEVO…MUEVO
mi cintura
to scare you.

And the Puente Prieto
torn down
and replaced by otro voto.

OBSERVING NATURE/RAGS TO RICHES

Castro dancing
el cha cha cha
with a bucket de
azúcar.

There's a tortuga, too,
para
carnalismo
pero camisa.

I discover myself carne-meat
en una
drugstore.
Hasta "La Causa"
is there!

La tierra supplies it
the sea where
we came from
riding en manteca-Apache.
Quien sabe más than
all of us put together
con una garra seeing the bubbles.

ALCATRAZ POLKA PINCHE

The stallions after
the Indians took over Alcatraz
estaban…Estevan…estaban…Estevan…
comiendo
duraznos during the rifles.

The so-called apalling, "Hey, vato…"
Zoot-Suit Riots
rompieron
the Navy destroyer como candy wrapper.

A truck bien lucas
en el barrio
leaping
como pachucos.

Y mi ruca
también fighting
for what belongs to her body.

Already una cosa becomes
a line in this poem trabajando
to sangre libre pertain.

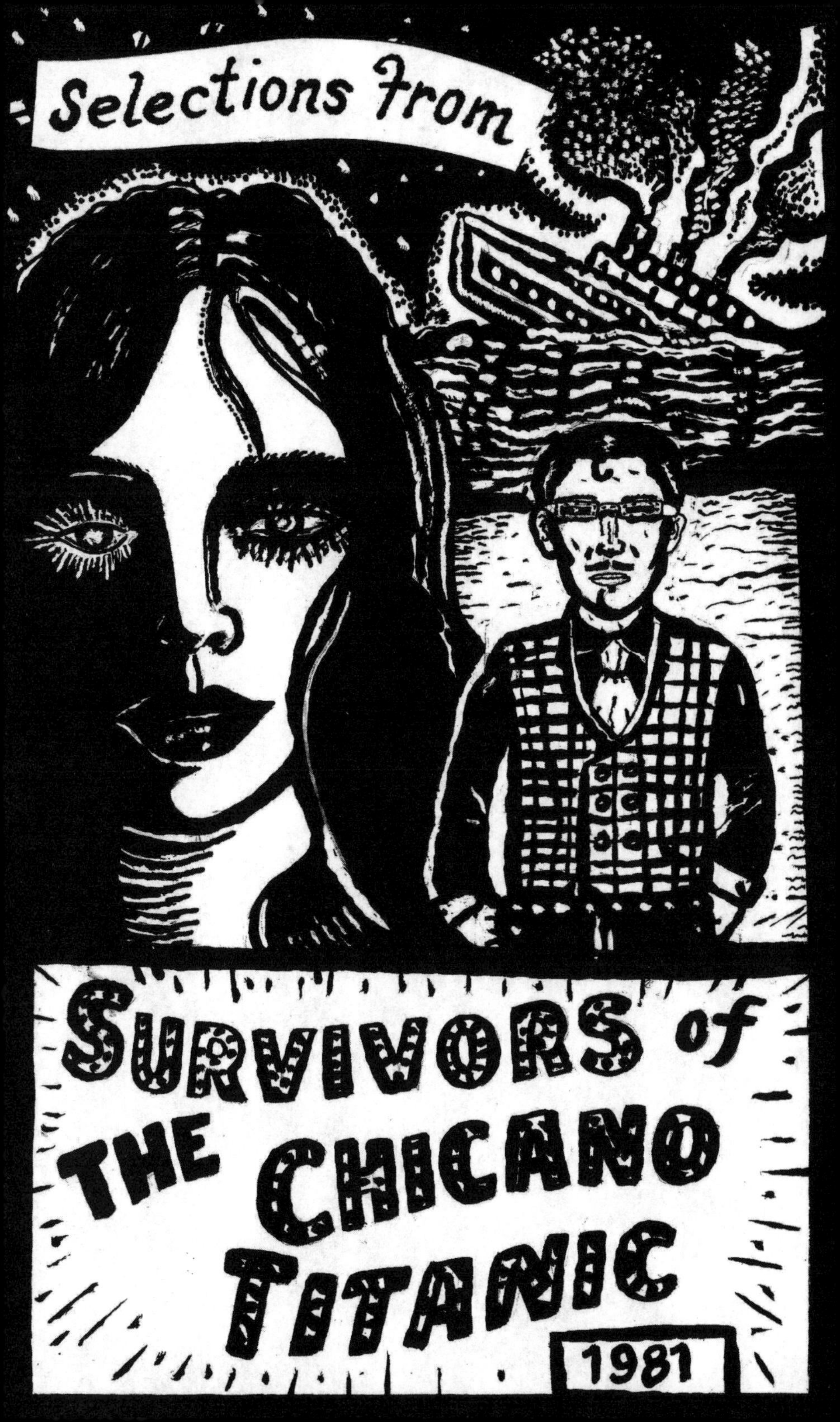
Selections from
SURVIVORS of THE CHICANO TITANIC
1981

SURVIVORS OF THE CHICANO TITANIC

The Titanic is
busy tonight.
Swirling out
of the fog.

Destiny, as
Huidobro said
in *Poemas Árticos*,
amounts
to mutilation.

Destiny, he said,
rates next
to DNA.

Last time
I saw him
he was wearing,
slovenly, a Chesterfield.

Sure, he was
one of the survivors.
That's all
there is.

Survivors have
that glint in their eyes.
That swaggered
humility.

If you lie
still, and breathe
calmly, you'll
float inside yourself.
And as far away
as Bermuda
the hats
are riding the waves in.

The biceps
in a King Kong movie,
stark images
against these
new arrivals.

INTIMIDATIONS

The bombs in
airport lockers
wag their tails,
the two loaves.

Truman Capote
on television
leans back
and comes back around.

Alright to leave
for Paris, and other parts
now that
Elridge Cleaver, pseudo-rebel,
like our forefathers
has returned.

Certainly, we can
never have enough.
We swallow fast,
and open the mouth,
deplore the minuses,
avoid crows
to the World Trade Towers.

The Statue
of Liberty
at the entrance
to tennis shoes,
welcoming
sex-change operations,
Arabs
with machine guns.

The world connotes,
pushes itself on you,
smiles terrible,
plays soccer,
has poets
with clubfeet
engage in incest.

It comes
back around
like Truman.

Trying to
catch his tail,
won't matter,
consaguinity's
too thick.

Stutters in front
of you,
embarrasses you,
exposes magenta!

Jim Morrison
waves his penis
at rock and roll
audiences.

All that
is gone;
hippies
leave San Francisco.
Even the Golden Gate Bridge.
Eyeglasses
on the faces
of Tokyo businessmen,
short little things.

Even the
cult of Godzilla,
drum majorette AWOL,
disconnect from reality,
like cannibals.

The river floats
face down,
centipede, Atlantis.

The death grip
never comes,
lies back waiting.
Hungry lights
powered by batteries now.

We keep
moving backwards.
Until we are
deep into it,
only as spiders
can we stand
the ocean pressure.

Well-rounded
creatures
so far from the Beatles,
from palliative,
we burst in on the sun.

The bombs
explode.
Lymph nodes
fall from heaven,
replace us well enough —
al least no one seems to notice.
No one is shocked
a foot away.

CARMEN

Why is the telephone such a donut, Carmen?
Next it will be the plaza
that cowers to
be alone.

And after that, I don't know,
maybe, the head shows,

seizes the future,
it all falls into place.

The freckles twirl away from your
shoulders like the universe.
I mean, they spin
a cocoon for a lozenge.

It's pried off.
Even the transistor radios.
But it's good to hear your knees
breathing so quietly in line...
A line of swimming pools.

A line, far away as Punta Arenas.
A pink monster dreamt by Neruda.
It's rubbish to think of it,
vagina, laundromat, coup d'etat,
like I said before, I don't know,
maybe it just keeps going.

Like being stuck to the wall
of injustice,
demure of poetic license,
peace nevertheless enters.

And, of course, peace
is only the start.
Yet, the flat world cannot scare you
with Italian cinema.

Nor can you drag your feet
over rock gardens,
past barrio dudes,
a bolt at your neck
like Frankenstein.

The German bakery
the Zoot-Suit riots,
finally the warning of donuts
to Don Juan.

An hourglass filled with glue.
The backbone
sliding in the arroyo.

Tenderness, and tenderness
begins buzzing over the cord
like tastebuds in the house.

And at dawn it is all over.
The guitar neck,
a San Andreas Fault
swallowing San Francisco:
lonely refrigerator.

These are our lives,
yours and mine,
following the coast-line,
sea-shell mongers, crab-like duties.

Sea-weed in the cauldron,
the long lonely beach, copy-catter
tries to catch its own tail,
yours, mine,
a shirt-tail,
Fonzie.

The San Andreas Fault
boarded up, deep ghetto,
stale jelly roll,
limp Dali cocks.

Afterbirth on the pier.
You see it swimming away,
sandwiches arrive,
a stingray doubles back…

Later, in your apartment
I see your face
ink-stained from writing so much.

FRUGALITY ON SIXTH STREET

Guilty guitars,
Mariachi dudes.
No tamales left
for *The Adventures of the Chicano Kid*
by Max.

Every Chicano
is in a wheelchair.
Aztlan becomes a foot
guided by toothpicks.

Sicily like
grandparents
gets inflated, bigger,
bigger, bigger.

The mutilation of Santos.
His previous smiles
make a small hill
outside Dallas.

The Goodyear blimp
behind La Malinche
looks like
a strike.

The nerve cells
bunch up,
crush each other
with Kleenex.

ELEGY FOR JOE CAMPOS TORRES

This Houston acropolis
in the pit
lionized into
likenesses.

It's not a stranger's wrist
handcuffed to this wrist,
it's someone very well
known to himself.

A few blocks away
a Jack-in-the-Box restaurant
stalagtites business
with Jesus Christ.

Nearby Galveston hotels
welcome the enemy…
An aloof political Mona Lisa
that never fails.

Yes, bury this talk
it never was an Astrodome.
Telephone Mickey Mouse
that it's over.

It was, after all,
pancakes not justice.
Just enough of them
dinosaur out to us somehow.

Just enough of them
to make us feel it,
a pain that we
try to put in the trash.

Even in the
swimming pool
if we can
but we can't.

There's really
no place for this pain,
it doesn't even
belong here.

THE DRAGONFLY

After Vallejo

This small dragonfly doesn't move anymore;
a mass of dryness cannot remind
us of blood.

I held it in my hand. Wings that could
have beat back any enemy.
I begin by seeing his eyes,
like those Cuauhtemoc must have had.

The grill of a car demands
at times a heavy price.
The beast intact, but its life in shambles.

The wings failed in a critical instant,
and he flew towards.
I regard it and wash away
the present for a moment.

This dragonfly that can't continue
one more step...
I think of countless zig-zags, turns, and dives,
and stare at the everlasting in its face.

POEMA SANDINO

estas cosas que nos arrastran por el piso
tenemos que pararlas como un árbol seco de navidad
tenemos que echarle agua hasta que le salgan hojas
hasta que podamos hablar otra vez
hasta que podamos mover al siglo
la cómoda que no nos deja abrir la puerta
el sofá roto que cubrimos con sábanas

este frío que nos tiene temblando día y noche
este granizo que entra por el techo
este sol dinerozo que quema la cabeza
tenemos que salirnos de la casa
para ya poder vivir en ella libres

2.

esta gente que no oye lo que pasa en el mundo
y aunque oiga, no le importa, no siente
no comprende que el mundo alcanza a todos

pero nosotros, nosotros tenemos que resistir al tiempo
levantar la pluma aunque sea con huesos
tenemos que ofender a los que cierran los ojos
que hasta páginas vacías ahoguen sus sueños dulces
que despiertan tosiendo buscando aire

ELEGY FOR
JOHN LENNON
1985

1. HORIZONTAL VIGNETTES OF THE
NAKED CITY

> *"I baked my first loaf of bread, and you can't*
> *believe how perfectly it rose. I've taken a*
> *Polaroid of it, and I think I can get it out to*
> *you by messenger tonight."*
> John in a telephone conversation with Elliot Mintz

On 42nd Street flesh becomes believable
through the pornographers' own credulity.
A pint that has, of all things,
been poodled by its owner
screeches to a halt.
Nearby, Delmore Schwartz once hid in his apartment,
concerned with the crud of his race;
John Berryman and others kept insisting,
"Go out and buy baloney, boy!"
In the Garment District
Mafia delivery trucks look ordinary.
And in front of The Dakota
the Beatles break up forever;
and Chapman tells reporters
from his jail cell, "Don't call me
Chapman, call me Chapstick…"

2. ROCK AROUND THE CLOCK

In his mind's eye Yoko and him
were indeed crucified
and, ironically, back in the Sixties
he once said that the Beatles
were more popular than Jesus Christ.
When John was living alone in Los Angeles
he taped a Kotex to his head
like a prescience of
his future house-husbandry.
So in 1975 John retired
to bake bread and raise Sean,
the only gurus he had time for

were Stratocaster, Gitanes and
fly-by-night 'round the world trips,
while he quietly plotted songs.
How and why had
Elvis Presley died in the Army?
Did Eleanor Rigby just have
a bad case of ramapithecus?
And now even though the deranged
Chapman has carried out his deed,
no one can ever really kill John.

3. THE GOOD, THE BAD AND THE UTOPIAN

John is alive and living in Argentina
(like they used to say of Hitler)
the Tai Chi, the torii
packed in Yoko's steamer trunks have joined them
in a Fifties-looking Buenos Aires,
all the Fords and Chevies
have wide whitewall tires.
The saxophone has not
yet been replaced by the guitar
as the prima donna of rock and roll.
The Beatnik snap of the fingers
has superceded applause…
it was then that
John took the ball
and ran with it.

4. THE MAGICAL MYSTERY TOUR

When acid rock was king
and The Thirteenth Floor Elevators
toured Texas like tornadoes,
John had become a sergeant.
A Spaniard had grown up
to hallucinate an imaginary world
in which peace and justice
actually existed.
A few years later, while reclining

in the Oval Office,
Nixon would tell his aides, "Fuck
the Constitution!" and eventually
Ford pardoned the fornication—
but the Magical Mystery Tour
stops only in Paradise.

5. SOME TIME IN THE NAKED CITY

The limousine pulls up outside the Dakota
and as John and Yoko walk
through the iron gates
a man calls, "Mr. Lennon."
The man smiles, then turns
and walks away.
In the White Room
John listens to a tape of Yoko's
"Walking On Thin Ice."
Gradually it begins to sink in, the electron is neither
particle nor wave, the *Best
of Carson* is on and
on another network
Howard staccatos *Monday Night Football.*

"THE BRITISH ARE COMING, THE BRITISH
ARE COMING!"

> *Being a remembrance of those
> days in the early Sixties when
> the phrase was applied to the
> invasion by British rock bands
> of U.S. air waves and the present
> day airs about Buenos Aires.*

When the General Belgrano went down
with the ease of the Spanish Armada
it seemed as if Margaret Thatcher was king again,
but a few days later,
when the HMS Sheffield was hit
by French-made missile,

everybody was proclaiming, Long Live The King.
We must remember (because we forget)
that little wars are made of larger lives.
Stonehenge, Martin Fierro,
come together in a way Beatle John Lennon
warned us to forego.
But, Las Malvinas Lonely Hearts Club Band
has hired a different drummer
and Ringo's been left out in the cold.

THE UNDEFEATED CHAMP

It's either Michael Jackson
or the Police that will inherit
John's championship belt
or so claims the rock and roll critics.
If the fools need glasses
Buddy's and John's are available.
There's more to the world
than beatings and synchronicity.
Maybe a bed-in for peace
won't really bring peace to the world
but neither will making
commercials for Pepsi
or acting in movies
set on some distant desert planet.

SAN LENNONISTA

When John flew into Athens
and realized he'd forgotten his LSD,
his aide-de-camp had to phone London
and tell them to air-mail the medicine
for John's "acidity."
The Beatles island
sprawled on the Aegean,
focused into utopia
by lash as need be—
the same sea Xerxes had whipped.
But eventually John
had to go back to being a Teddy Boy

because you can't pull punches
and remain the champ.

ELEGY FOR SYLVIA PLATH

The Beatles came upon the music scene
just a little too late to save you Sylvia.
The British Invasion that brought us
the Stones, the Dave Clark Five,
Freddie and the Dreamers,
Gerry and the Pacemakers,
Petula Clark, the Kinks
and of course your saviours
who unfortunately arrived a couple of years
too late to do American literary history
any good…you could have
spared yourself if you had stuck
your head inside of Donovan instead.

THE NEXT BIG THING

At the height of their fame
when not even thick walls of lead
could keep out Beatlemania,
the Beatles flew off to India
seeking the enlightenment of the Maharishi.
John vacillated between
a hundred percent
and a hundred and ten percent.
But in a few weeks
he was back with Cynthia,
or was it with Yoko?
Dylan introduced the Beatles
to marijuana in New York City.
After that, Paul couldn't ever do without it,
no matter how many times he was busted.

1. THE THIRTEEN CALUMNIES

> *"Hello, daddy, I just shot Jodie Foster,*
> *can I come home?"*
> Aron Latham in "The Dark Side
> of the American Dream," RS 375

If all Hinckley wanted
was Jodie Foster's attentiona
not even a pro could have done a better job.
The President being shoved into a Lincoln
on national television,
a bullet lodged in his lung.
Later from his jail cell
Hinckley threatens to rape her, to kill her...
he claims he would have killed Lennon
if Chapman hadn't beat him to the punch —
which serves to remind us that nuts
belong behind bars
or at least in the trees
with the hominid ancestors of man
(where natural selection would have rooted them out).

2. THE DARWINESE MOVIEGOER

> *"Hello, daddy, I've just been shot.*
> *Please call an ambulance!"*
> Hinckley after being shot
> to death by Chapman

They ought to put Hinckley
and Chapman in the same cell,
let them take out their
misanthropic violence against each other.
Let them start out with knives,
machetes, bows and arrows,
and in the end, let them
blow each other's brains out.
That way Jodie can finish
college in relative safety
and can go on to make movies
or host *Saturday Night Live*.

THE DAY UNDONE

The bullets flew out of his body
and back into the pistol
and Mark David Chapman

pulled the bullets from the chamber,
subwayed his crazy ass home,
never got the autograph,

never talked to John at all.
This is the moment that really belongs
in the Rock and Roll Hall of Fame

and not this sick bastard
trying to visit his parents,
his psychoanalyzed mind

still outsmarted by watermelon rinds,
putrid on the best New Jersey street
as he shuffled his slimy feet

on his way to Bethlehem
to be aborted
on the day undone.

SURFING DOWN MEMORY LANE

The surfer songs echo
like the percussion of the sea.
It doesn't matter that the Beach Boys
are over forty now
and that the polka dot bikinis
have lain moth-eaten for two decades
or that an occasional hippie
pops up out of nowhere
incredible as that may sound.
Today even the pop music
of Australia is tinged with reggae
and the squalid poverty of Kingston
has spread to the affluent suburbs.

BARBAROUS END

Dennis was the only surfer
in the bunch yet somehow
they gave us Frankie and Annette
and kept America happily beachcombing,
at least, until the Beatles came along.
But, this week it all
came to an end for Dennis,
yesterday the Coast Guard buried him at sea
strapped to a surfboard
like the early short-haired Sixties.

CHILDE-CAMPESINO

A smoke-filled room
in which a man contemplates the Fifties,
the migrant worker days of cotton pickers
and pecan gatherers, sweating
side by side with braceros.
The taste of sweetrolls
in a Roscoe, Texas café and the oil derrick
on the farmhouse backyard
and the Lubbock elementary school cafeteria
chocolate milk
race towards Seguin like
a blue norther. Richard
Nixon was only Vice-
President then
and Buddy Holly struggled
hard as hell to perfect
a beady-eyed rock and roll.

RUN SILENT, RUN DEEP

A brand new (1957) white Ford Thunderbird
passes our submarine-like Studebaker at light speed
(sonar can't detect us on Route 2)
and since I didn't know any English
I couldn't understand

the slurred speech of Marlon Brando
in *The Wild One* or the words
of Lash LaRue…yang was pitted
against Beatnik (as I've come to realize
only now) and the Eisenhower crew-cut
defined black and white television
as it has never been defined since.

THE WHITE HOUSE INN

The car-hops at the White House Drive Inn
were never really pretty, the neon lights atop
the Fifties architecture
flashed from bright to gray.
On Saturday nights (after a dance
or a movie at the Dixie) the cars
circled endlessly around
or finally stopped.
If I think about it now
a few stray memories come to mind,
one of the De Leones got shot there
in a drunken gunfight
and Larry Nieto could
play pinball all night long.
But sometime in the early Seventies
the White House was torn down
and a convenience store was put in its place,
the elater twisted slowly
until only the new was left.

FOSSIL CHICANICUS

This is a vague reconstruction
of Juan Seguín Elementary School
back in 1955 or thereabouts.
My first love was a girl named Carmen,
I was madly in love with her
until I turned sixteen.
I always walked behind her
after school

and for some reason I still recall
staring at her TV antennae
atop her house.
As the front door closed behind her
I kept on walking
the two miles to the farm
to eat cold beans from the pot.

COMING OF AGE IN THE SPACE AGE

The V-2's weren't that impressive
except in the science fiction movies of the Fifties
when they suddenly became rocket ships
to Mars or Venus.
The Mercury program barely
earned its feathered heel,
yet rocketed NASA to fame somehow.
And if the figures are correct,
of those coming of age
in the space age, everybody made it
except of course the three in the Apollo module
that was sitting on the ground
and a few unlucky cosmonauts.

CHICANO TEENS (OF TWENTY YEARS AGO)

It wasn't really that long ago
I was dancing to The Swim with Minga
in the summer of 1964
somewhere in Highland Hills.
If we stared towards downtown
we could see the workmen
busy atop the Tower of the Americas
(it was under construction).
You couldn't hear anything
on KTSA except the Beatles.
A day before he got shot
we saw Kennedy's motorcade
in front of Brooks Air Force Base.
During his speech his voice echoed

with the aid of loudspeakers
and carried across to the tubercular hospital.
He was talking about the moon.

SPEED OF LIGHT

A hurried kiss on a college parking lot
and the heartbeat becomes sevenfold,
like the number of seas,
or like the theories of the moon's creation,
though only two are much discussed.
Was it created from debris
left after the earth was formed,
or is it one of Velikovsky's comets
captured like Venus?
You get into your car
like Ingrid Bergman,
the propellers cut through
emotions that are larger than life,
but the silver screen
has been replaced by the boob tube.

RUSO

Another theory about the moon's origin
has it being captured by Mars,
and then after all life ended there,
the moon (our present moon) found its way here.
Some say it gave rise
to woman's intuition,
and that before the moon arrived
women did not menstruate.
Some men like Li Po
and the American astronauts died in its pursuit,
buried in a capsule
like Buddhist monks
protesting the Asian War,
or like Gagarin
knowing Russia had no chance at all.

HISTORY

The Moonglows were an early Sixties
San Antonio Tex-Mex band,
years of eclipse, and even snow
this far south, and a time
to speculate about going to the moon.
Back then only Popeye
could put a man in orbit (poor Bruto),
though Wells of course had been
there and back in the 19th century.
He had even been there
when the barbarians
invaded Europe like the unknown Beatles.

CURTAINS

Plath, too, was in Europe in the early Sixties,
writing like Sappho, but with a twist,
here chubby kids growing
along with the Iron Curtain
and the number of military advisors
in Southeast Asia, growing along
with the Russian space program
while Kennedy flew down to Dallas,
or to da'las to be more exact.
Chuck Yeager had dreamt
of going places too,
but on his own, piloting his own ship
roaring over the mountains of the moon
and landing in some valley,
drinking a beer and flying back.

WOMAN

It is not the moon, but you, woman,
who make the whitecaps
and the earth bulge
at the equator, and you
who try to make sense

out of the madness of the world.
It is you who takes the bull by the horns
on the Minoan palace walls,
beside the dolphins
which are supposed to be our cousins —
they've been known to save man,
though they cannot save him from himself,
and woman can only save so much.

LINES

You rearranged pebbles on the Nazca plain,
from your hands were born birds and spiders,
and supposedly air fields
for ancient UFO's, ships no doubt manned
by australopithecus venusian.
You kept Macchu Picchu clean
while at the same time
predicting and assuring its future —
though only the genes
of that future exist,
their whereabouts can't ever be ascertained.
And it was you who baked
the clay toy airplanes that intrigue us today.

CAVEAT EMPTOR

Columbus (not Columbia) started off badly, too,
he almost had to walk (God forbid) to the Indies
and then, though he discovered a new continent,
he died not knowing it.
So beware when you finally do blast off,
don't find a Mother Ship orbiting earth,
or Haley's comet heading straight for us.
And about the miracle drugs
that can only be manufactured in space,
once you get back down
don't hand them over to the drug companies —
they'll just pass on the cost
of the entire Shuttle to the consumer.

CHICANO IN THE SHUTTLE

1. EL BENNY CHUNIAR

I look for my barrio from a hundred miles up
but earth has become one,
like a statue of an Etruscan couple,
serene, confident and eternal.
The red white and blue
turns green white and blue with a field of real stars
dominating the black background of space.
The inexplicable quasars
recede like peace.
Lebanon and El Salvador
and all the other trouble spots on earth
where people kill each other
look uninhabited.

2. I LOOK DOWN AT THE VALLEY

I look down at the Valley
but campesinos and lowriders
must be keeping a low profile.
I don't see any pintos either
but I know they
didn't go anywhere.
I don't see unwed mothers
nor mothers on welfare.
I don't see little kids
running around shirtless
in public housing
but they must be there.

LITTLE EVA

The records, late Fifties stuff,
rekindle old fires
and the autodidactic learns
that the Sumerian word ti

means both "life" and "rib"
so he can't help noting
that the Spanish word "costillas"
also means ribs.
They stick out of Eve
like a sore thumb —
the forbidden fruit
with bobby socks around the ankles.

THE FOUR DIRECTIONS

The Sue Thompson 45
spins round and round
until its trombones dominate the landscape
like a smaller oom pah pah.
The ancient grooves
wind down to a black hole
and perhaps because of the
magnetized iron deposits
in the human sinus bones
the needle drags the music
out of us like north.

THE FOUR PITHECUS

1. THE STONE AGE

The bitumen can't possibly get out of place
like the Shirelles' stiff
Adorn-sprayed hairstyle.
The Cuban missile crisis
suffered a fate worse than the Big Bopper
and Kennedy slumped over in the back seat.
I myself went to sleep
in science class
while the Acid Age failed
to respond to Rolaids,
the Stone Age itself
ignored rock and roll

though the finny radio was tuned
to the popular hits of the day.

2. THE FAB FOUR

The past comes apart like a burlap sack
left too long on the ground,
black and white TV was king
and Elvis wasn't even a close second.
The radio spilled over
into de-segregation.
Fats Domino and Little Richard
bobbed like apples behind the piano
and the future President
was still a Senator.
Years later Leonov walked in outer space
just as I strayed into junior high.

FIFTY DAYS AND FIFTY NIGHTS

Loveless and limbless on a flood plain,
the ears pinned back,
the hair in a Fifties crew cut.
Fats Domino, gas stations giving away
tumblers with a fill-up of gas, Bobby Rydell,
Cold War, bobby socks, anything and
everything left dinosaur footprints.
There is more treasure here
than in the Rift Valley of Africa,
rockabilly rivals Australopithecus
and the Stone Age is still
in the very distant future.
I wear khaki pants and T-shirt,
drink beer in the restrooms
of the Royal Sports dancehall,
then I go out and look across the dance floor
at my childhood sweetheart—
the floor sweeps everything away.

DON'T FORGET THE FIFTIES

Can't co-existence with women
be classified along with
the Eisenhower years as fodder
for the Cold War? Yet, you give me
the cold shoulder as if
Victorian values had proved
undependable buffers…
"Oh, darling, don't forget that
bobby socks and pompadours
generated the Bristol Stomp
and that Rosie and the Originals
crooned 'My Angel Baby'
on a Protestant American Bandstand,
don't forget that the libido
took a licking which was justified
only because there was no justice."

SMALL STILL-LIFE OF THE SIXTIES

The Four Tops do their dance routine
while they lip-sync
their hits on American TV
and no one notices
a handful of military advisors
landing in the early Sixties Saigon.
Soon Frankie and Annette
plunge into their Beach Party movies.
Elvis counter-attacks
with Fort Lauderdale.

SPACE: THE FUMBLED FRONTIER

1. MAN OF THE MOON

The heat-shield held and Glenn
made it back to earth safely,
three orbits for the military-industrial complex

with a ticker-tape parade in New York City
thrown in to rival his rivals.
Maybe the whole thing
won't really work according to plan,
that is, John going from test pilot to President,
but NASA is already (secretly, of course)
planning to send him up
in one of the future Shuttles,
hoping that if he gets elected
its own reward will be astronomical.

2. EVENING NEWS

In Peking the Chinese have slaughtered
two-hundred thousand dogs in the last two days
and from the Space Shuttle
the angry voice of an astronaut
castigates ground control.
How quickly the beauty of space
succumbs to that of the down-to-earth,
or was it just some wise guy
imitating Chuck Yeager?
In Washington the Reagan Administration
says it can't attach any strings
to the military aid it gives
to the government of El Salvador,
"Human rights," the spokesman says "must sometimes
take a back seat to democracy."

3. CHARIOTS OF THE MINOR GODS

If Kennedy was alive today
he certainly would have found a way
to get himself aboard the Shuttle.
His book about his Presidency
would be a bestseller
in spite of the supposed shenanigans.
But none of this will come to pass
and one can imagine
Jackie in outer space or confirming

stories about John to the *National Enquirer*.
Indeed, the New Frontier is rather old now,
the space program itself has shown
that we can't escape the gravity of earth.

SCOTCH ME UP, BEAMY

As soon as the brothers landed,
the military was waiting with ideas of their own
and the space program is no different;
the CIA commandeers Columbia
and Enterprise to try out
its "Star Wars" weapons.
But the worst part is
that whenever an astronaut
opens his or her mouth,
they sound like some redneck Texan.
There's no Captain Kirk type,
no Bones (not Berryman's), no Spock,
only ray-gun toting gringos and vendidos.

UHURA

Through Women in Action you put Sally in space,
after all those years of having
a silver little bugger in your ear
communicating with the Federation;
black as the freedom of space
you sat by the console
in your short skirt,
knees together even at warp nine.
You recruited Sally
and she became the first
American woman in space,
which proves that courtship
bows to spaceship
and muscle-boundness lies astern.

THAT'S ALL VOLKS

The subliminal racism of a man named White
being the first American to walk in space
can't be undone by Svetlana.
Though she's been out there before,
this time she becomes a Soyuz herself,
tumbling towards earth,
gazing at the icy fences of Siberia.
The mysterious turn of the century
explosion burned a forest or a nation—
from this far up nothing is definite.
Svetlana's curves are hidden in her suit,
and as she climbs back in,
her comrades seem surprised
that the moon did not abduct her.

SPACE

1. THE FINAL FRONTIER

They say the first woman in space
was incompetent and sick throughout the mission
and that the second one
was a hell of a cosmonaut.
Now the first American woman
is circling earth at a dizzy pace,
an astrophysicist by profession,
female by chromosomal chance.
Even Gloria Steinem strutted
by the launch pad to see her off,
rocket fuel lighting up the day
and G-forces building up like history.
You've come a long way, baby,
and you don't even smoke.

2. FIRST THINGS FIRST

Supposedly the Russians got the best

of the German rocket scientists
and that's why they beat
the Americans into outer space,
put the first satellite out there,
the first dog, first man, first woman,
and just barely failed in putting
a communist on the moon.
Finally, twenty years after Mercury,
Sally orbits round and round in Challenger.
Her husband down on earth
jealous not of men but of space.

3. APPLIED SCI-FI?

And of what benefit is it?
Sally floating around in shorts
in the cockpit, releasing two satellites
and baby-sitting a medical experiment
that can only be carried out in zero gee
while below in the center of the Gulf of Mexico
a low-pressure area fills up with clouds.
El Salvador is clear
and Green Berets are nowhere
evident in Honduras
nor Contras further south.
And Asimov opines on television,
"Perhaps the benefits of all this
will prove retroactive."

ADAMSKI & EVE

1. MOST OF US,

unfortunately cannot venture like Adamski
into the cylindrical or even step in orbit,
releasing, retrieving, releasing
and retrieving some satellite,
origin German, Indonesian, except Pago Pago, etc.
Christ! jellybeans in zero gee

instantly become diet jelly beans.
There's also a wonderful view of earth,
the horn of Africa silent,
the stubble of astronaut chins
and of at least one pair of shins.
Would Kennedy have invited her to the White House
and then turned on the Kennedy charm?

2. CHALLENGER IS SUPPOSED

to enter the atmosphere over Hawaii,
proceed northeast, cross over northern Mexico,
over Texas, the guys and gal will wave
howdy to the Johnson Space Center
(old Lyndon packed all the fringe benefits
he could into his home state)
and then slice along to the Cape.
This is of course a far cry
from *Inside The Flying Saucers*
or from benevolent Klaatu.
H.G. Wells sent his own Gravy Train to the moon,
breaking the natural laws that man
has forced upon the universe.
If Neil Armstrong took a giant step
forward for mankind,
was Sally's step petit?

3. SOFTWARE

On the average they wear a smaller
size shoe and in character more gothic,
the pointed high heels could bludgeon,
or simple white sandals resemble orchids,
the thin white straps winding like tendrils.
In tube tops or
low-cut evening gown,
in faded blue jean cut-offs,
the subtraction becomes addition.
Robbed of eye-shadow and lipstick
for a moment in space,

timing the launch around menstruation
lest cramps interfere with onboard computers —
the purely macho inanities
may just be worth the mission.

CASABLANCA

1. IN THIS LOVE AFFAIR OF THEIRS

In this love affair of theirs
he likes to box back half her ears,
their future, like the Grand Canal,
is very nervous about it.
Fists as flashy
as the black ships
that hovered on the Japanese horizon.
They follow the hickeys on her neck,
the small clots in fatigues
and like the war over the Falkland Islands
they get so close to *The Thing*
(the one with James Arness) and so
damn close to the Exocet and the Buenos Aires
gangsters of the Forties and Fifties
who've turned terrorists or rightist military now.
Fernando Lamas dies of cancer
during one of their rows.

2. RUNWAY 00ZILCH

The propellers cut through fog
and the goodbye kiss lies on the runway
like peanuts, Morocco chained
to West Africa.
The figures wearing the Sahara-like gloves,
the Desert Fox at the other end.
So it is not surprising
that the hominids Leakey found
detective us from jungle
to concrete jungle.

Could we (if we really had to)
handle a stone tool?
Outrun an antelope on the savanna,
cut sinew from bone with a scraper?
In a tangle with Nazis
anything would be a good idea.

3. THE SWING ERA

They won't understand this in Tibet,
no, they won't understand it at all.
Glenn Miller wouldn't hear of it
adrift in the English Channel.
German prisoners of war
carved exotic pipes in West Texas,
time multiplies and yet remains sterile.
Bogie's basset hound eyes
went well with gangsters
and Hemingway novels.
Yet, in the end, no matter
how great a sacrifice it may appear,
letting a loved one go not only flatters the age
but leaves nothing for the next one.

4. PHOENIX

There's a vast difference between
the U-boat aficionados and the Love Boat Lothario,
the most obvious being forty years.
If any couple kicked out of paradise
put up a fight
surely Eva and Adolph
fought just as hard as any other
like Bogie and Bacall
did in the Fifties.
But then Elvis Presley
sprang up out of the ashes,
out of black blues roots.
The hillbilly rockabilly
sound did away with the he-man.

After all, a culture does not live
by cinematic art alone,
at least, not until
what once ended up on the cutting room floor
winds up in Washington.

5. B-CUP MOVIES

In his last movie
Reagan played the part of a thug
who beat up Angie Dickinson,
or was it Emily Dickinson?
The bad acting hurt
more than the black eye.
When Bogie beat a woman
she was supposed to enjoy it.
Her orgasm would
ignore the director.
There's a man in *Casablanca*
and no man in the White House
so a lover's spat in the Rose Garden
ends up with Nancy frustrated,
unfrigged and faultless
even on their California ranch.

6. NEANDERTHAL WOMAN

Making love with her
was an evolutionary dead end.
Perhaps the chromosomes,
surmised the horses heads,
did not reach towards immortality
(immorality maybe).
Was it Bogie or John Wayne
who smoked Camels
to the bitter end?
But it wasn't smoke, it was fog,
the DC-3 is snappily romantic
but solely from a contemporary point of view.
Today, old "Play It Again, Sam"

and a fleet of pianos
could not revive the institution.
Only uniqueness can ever be unique again.

ELEGY FOR JAMES WRIGHT

What was it the young critic Jonathan Cott
said of you during the Sixties,
something about Sung sensibility,
not to mention Sioux brave bravado.
In one of your elegies you see
the bear Ted Roethke
by the bedside of another dying poet,
but there are no pagodas or teepees
in your real life, only the dark America
that strikes out at tolerance.
Drunk like Li Po you could have drowned
in the reflection of the moon
but it was occupied by NASA.

EPILOGUE: POETIC JUSTICE

1. THESE ARE THE WEAKNESSES OF POETS

These are the weaknesses of poets.
Berryman couldn't bridge the gap,
Delmore refused to leave
his cheap New York hotel.
Hart Crane gaily disappeared
in the Bermuda Triangle.
Merton electrified us all.
Neruda was killed
by an American junta
and Lowell died in a taxi
en route to his own death.

2. GLACIER NATIONAL POET

You plowed right through the ice,
your thinning hair focused
on the mantle of the Mississippi.
You were still mumbling to the honky Sambo
that you made a hero,
you had much in common
with the uncommon,
though in that, of course, you were like most poets.
But you didn't have to go
to such extremes,
Frost was only joking
about favoring ice.

3. INKFISH

In the hit movie *Splash*, Darryl Hannah
plays the part of a mermaid
who falls in love with a human,
a human whom she had met
when they were both children.
I hope you weren't expecting
her to save your skin, John.
Or (and this is more likely) maybe you thought
Lloyd Bridges in his old *Seahunt*
television role was down there
with an extra tank for you?
Ironically, it was Henry
who reeled you in.

ELEGY FOR BUDDY HOLLY

1. PEGGY SUE

When Buddy looked out the window
and saw the ground racing towards him
he clutched at his guitar
but somebody pulled the plug anyway.

The crew-cuts on the Texas Tech campus
were barely aware of Pliny The Elder
but apparently knew "Peggy Sue" by heart.
All the copper in Makan
went into the pretty penny
that the dinosauric music industry
could get its hands on.
Colonel Parker was making
the Army work wonders for the King.
But when Buddy's plane hit the ground
it struck discord into the instrument
that would spread beyond the Sixties.

2. EYEGLASSES

The abdomen is the last to know
that the attainment can not rectify
the failure of an engine in a storm,
the lightning flashes in Buddy's face
and thunder drowns out the radio.
Decades later his eyeglasses
are found in some
personal property room
that some corrupt sheriff
had forgotten about,
forgotten like all the political prisoners
of modern states—
remembered like Lennon's shattered glasses
on the cover of a rock and roll album.
Maybe rock stars should stick
to wearing contact lenses.

3. KKK

What can be seen should
(by all accounts) be heard also,
the ebb and flow should obviously flow.
And even though Buddy
dropped out of the Space Age
quite too early,
the Space Age has gone back into

the past of its own accord. The
Sputnik beats America again and
Eisenhower summons
his barber twice a day.
But back in the present,
Lubbock and the rest of the state
nurture Klan-like ideals.

4. ROCKABILLY POLITICS

When Buddy got in his jalopy
he headed towards the
mom and pop convenient store
(which was convenient for America at the time).
He bought the Rainbow Bread
which was advertised on
the store's screen door
as being good bread,
an ice cold strawberry
Hippo soda water
which tasted immaculately great
even though Castro was doing
horrid things to Cuba said Uncle Sam.
Somehow rock and roll survived communism
and may yet survive democracy.

EPILOGUE TO AN AGE

CASABLANCA

It's eighty degrees in the middle of winter,
the theory of relativity excludes the in-laws.
The drug lords rule Colombia
with a no-look pass to Peru,
and slam dunk it in America's face.
When Zsa Zsa slaps a Hollywood cop,
the big pussy writes her a ticket
and becomes famous overnight.
We cannot understand

what we cannot understand,
the Buddha did not delve into Greek,
or the repair of trucks,
but we must let it go at that —
this plane lock Zen koan
has no answer in common speak.
I wear my hair like a charro,
knowledge crunching from news
of the world, my white shirt
spiraling like words on the page.
The cliff of my hometown is poetry
to the hunter and the hunted.
The syrup of truth
does not stick to our little Aztec bakery.
Stars glitter and evaporate
while Atlas holds Texas over his head —
this rarefied air makes rednecks of us all.
The Johnson Space Center
launches its cowpies into degenerate orbit,
and I drive around the four-cornered plaza
in my pickup truck like a toy.
My three arrogant chest hairs
venomous to the non-poet,
the chicken-sized Texas dinosaur,
stalactites in Tex-Mex food,
the Three Stooges take the place
of three of my tires,
and one of my books serves as the other.
Texas can still screw Alaska,
but not in the back of my truck!
Like they say, "Size isn't everything."
Kennedy dead in Dallas
with the Alamo stuck in his ass.
My white shirt x-rays the Gulf of Mexico
looking for the tattoo of dawn.
The skeletons of fish slump
but remain in their seats.
The Harbor Bridge above Corpus Christi
overlooks the carpentry of mankind,
armadillo of our fleshy armor
pinned to a bulletin board,
ignoring communication from floppy disk.

We play Thermopylae
to cushion us from Amtrak,
the heroes of independence
drink the National Beer of Texas
and step out of character
to leak Rio Bravo from open toga.
From the guru of Padre Island
Ghandi would not ask freedom,
the little glasses knife from his face,
windsurfers cloud the waves.
I turn forty-two and govern
the angry mob with an angry mob,
East and West become one,
our better half has gone on vacation.
Hawaii rises out of the Pacific like a nickel on
Marilyn Monroe's pubic hair.
Pearl Harbor burns until
lions reproduce on the beach,
giant yellow spots
cannot darken sunrise.
The lessons I learn
lean into the sky like bell towers.
In the anesthesia
of having been a rebel all my life
I will not sweek a truce.
I become Humphrey Bogart
completely myself in *Casablanca*
wearing my white dinner jacket,
double-breasted and one hundred percent silk.
But our modern day Nazis
star in much less famous movies,
their Volkswagens are made
in Mexico now.
Our present enemies
create Hiroshima in the cafe.
Mercury knowledge bananas
on the hillsides of Mt. Everest.
China uses Tibet as a paperweight.
The prayer wheels fall like snowflakes
on the Dalai Lama.
The poetry of Bogart's face
shimmering from a Sahara mirage.

I walk the streets of my town
in blue jeans and white shirt,
waging war against war,
against squares and hippies,
against hard rock and country music,
against atheists and Jehovah's Witnesses,
against vegetarians and carnivores,
against bicycles and the Concorde.
I go into the 50's style snack bar
at Lehmann's Drugstore,
achieve satori drinking Dr. Pepper.
Outside, sunshine confetti,
the mild winter red like a cherry.
Love ripples on Lake McQueeney
overturning boats and turtles,
the ripples spread to the land,
its atoms with holes in
the center like donuts.
My publisher has run off
to Sri Lanka
in search of giant Buddhas.
Driving an Austin cab
never made him a shaman.
I bet they don't serve tamales
in Colombo (the
capital, not the detective).
I bet he sits in
the lotus position
for an hour every day.
His mind becomes blank,
not from meditation,
but from brain damage.
He reads the
electrifying works of Merton
by lamp light
in the humid jungle.
The flora and the fauna breed
a thick coat of nothingness.
Nirvana cannot scale
anything higher than itself.
The island must tectonically
slam into the Himalayas some day

and my publisher,
if he's still there,
will be squashed.
But even then,
his creativity may not peak.
In nearby Bangladesh
no one cares about plate tectonics,
only about what's on the plate.
The Ganges gangs up
on residents to no avail.
Indiana Jones rafts down
one of the ice-cold rivers
in the upper foothills
unaware that satisfaction
can never be a fact.
The yeti's shit is flown to London
and I can't even afford
to teleport to California.
I could not witness
John Lennon's escapes in L.A.,
L.A. where even space junk
is worshipped.
Dodger Stadium flies
incoherent in the face,
Hollywood picks up its skirt
for everybody to see.
If Howard Hughes
was alive today
he'd make the Spruce Goose
out of sausage.
Pollution would zero in on clean air.
Disneyland would never grow up.
Some famous teenage girl
sings her hit songs in the malls
of the country.
Columbia flies in circles
around the troubled earth.
Amazon forests are cut away,
the silt oozes out
half-way into the Atlantic waters,
circling the island
where Napoleon was imprisoned.

The Count of Monte Cristo
slamming his fists against
the stone walls,
stones brought from northern Italy.
Great art destroyed by the Church.
I listen to eleven-year-old records
of the rock group The Police,
some song about a guerrilla girl.
She makes the same mistake
over and over again like me.
War is not hell, she says,
it is stupid. But since when
do women have a chance
to do anything about it?
Real life is so different
from what we want it to be,
the wrong people always win.
The barbarians, the Vandals,
the Gauls, the Russians,
the Americans, the bad guys.
My own hard rock guerrilla girl
out in East Texas,
lost in the thirteen Mexican rivers,
battling industrial toxins...
the honeymoon words
have no keyboard.
The Sabine full of wood shavings
suspended in Jello.
Your poetry fighting the past,
clubbing bright sun with thighs
until the Gulf becomes a pancake,
to be eaten, to be tossed
like a Frisbee, to be sailed
by Cola de Vaca, to be covered
in cellophane, your pen
finally out of ink,
the coast of Texas upside-down
on your little finger.
You tell me I'm obsessed
with *Casablanca* and its meanings,
you say I make its story

the story of you and me.
Even my '72 Dodge is parked
outside of Café Americain,
its aerodynamic ground effects
sleek in desert asphalt,
annihilating the distance
between here and Timbuktu.
But you fly off back to Groves
while I stay here
in rotten language of my town,
in the modern day language,
in the Stonehenge of landfills.
The Germans try to unite,
the Russians try to go their own way,
the Mexicans ruminate
in the middle of their minds.
Far away in Egypt,
waters behind the Aswan Dam
pile up until they back up
into the Antarctic mountains,
penguins flee, scientists
head back to their home countries
with the astounding news.
South of Casablanca in South Africa,
Mandela is a free man after 27 years,
but of course after 27 years in prison
nobody is a free man. And after
forty-two years of American freedom,
I am not free, you are not free,
we are not free.
As I cruise around town in my verse
in reverse, this is not *Casablanca*.
Time is not time, seconds are not seconds.
The plane carrying
the love of my life flies off
to the Azores to refuel.
And fifty years later,
the two Germanys reunite.
The Berlin Wall comes tumbling down
like an aftershock of the Frisco quake,

the Soviet bloc comes apart
like Lego blocks...
I sit down to meditate in the middle of winter
and I round up the usual suspects.

January 11, 1990

SELECTIONS FROM
I WAS NEVER A
MILITANT CHICANO

1986

IF WE PRAISE THE AZTECS

If we praise the Aztecs
or Zapata
we praise something
too far removed.
If we embrace Guevara
we must realize
that revolution
works only on rare occasions.
If we succumb
to the Great White Way
we learn the hard way.
If we try "the middle of the road"
we cross the
dividing line.
If we live for the future
we betray the present.
There's only one way
to go about it
so why put it off
any longer?

CHICANO BURGLAR

The Chicano burglar
gets 99 years
while the rich swindler
who operated his
crooked business
here in Seguin
gets off with a slap
on the wrist;
the lady down the street
has three little kids
no child support
works at the grocery store
makes three thiry-five
an hour
can't pay the bills
waits as a white woman

writes out a check
for groceries and a copy
of *People* magazine;
the boy
follows her
with her bags
out to the new Mercedes,
the well-groomed
white poodle
jumps up and down
when it sees its mistress.
The lady does not
tip the boy.
This is what this country
is all about,
if you are rich
you are equal to other rich people;
if you are poor
you are equal to other poor people.

THE POET'S BIRTHDAY

Today I am thirty-eight
my hair has become white
my politics
have become non-political,
the left and right
oppose me,
the violent inherit violence
and the meek
inherit meekness.
Ten years ago
I thought
there could be an answer
but it seems that
innocence and
loss of innocence
are the same thing.
The path to wisdom
is followed
not even by the wise

and no one is free
to travel
the road of freedom.
Today I am thirty-eight
and I no longer
ask any questions.
I should be
like a lyric
in one of
Víctor Jara's
songs of protest.
Instead I am like
the military
and the guerrillas,
always seeking the
unattainable.
But today I am thirty-eight,
I gnaw at time;
and if by chance
a little injustice
crumbles somewhere
on earth today,
then I celebrate.
If somewhere on earth
someone becomes more human today,
then I celebrate.
And if it's me
who becomes more human,
then I celebrate
even more.

I WAS NEVER A MILITANT CHICANO

I was never
like El Louie
and I am not Joaquín,
I never had
to worry
about surviving
in my barrio;
I never had

the driving force
to create
The Crusade for Justice
like Corky Gonzales,
I could never be
a César Chávez,
and reach down
deep inside
the earth
to find that
awesome inner strength.
Some of us
are just unable
to sacrifice ourselves.
I was never
like Raul Salinas,
alurista or Ricardo Sánchez
creating a new
world of poetry
out of a white wasteland.
Some are leaders
and creators,
some are followers,
but the followers want
justice and liberty
and fairness, too.
I could never
shout like Tigre.
But inside
(right here)
I guess I can
roar just as loud.
I never shot up
a federal courthouse
like Reies Tijerina
but I know
that the frustrations
won't stay
locked up forever.
I was never
really a pachuco
but I saw then what I still

see now —
that we're
getting nowhere,
that things
are worse
than they were
in the forties.
I was never
the Che Guevara-type
but there's
nothing wrong
with revolution.
Everybody says
it can't happen here,
but, hell,
it can happen anywhere.
I was never
a militant Chicano
but only because
I've always wanted
more than a revolution
can provide.

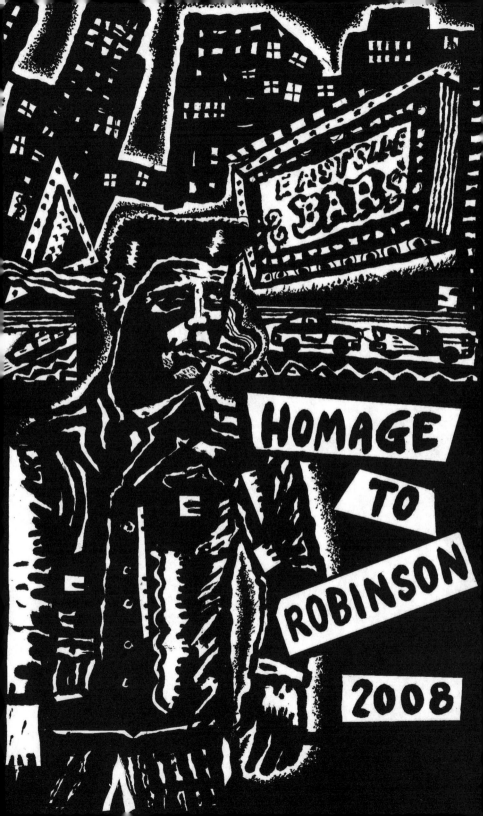

THE CITY DAMNED

With Ann naked in bed
Robinson stared out the window
at the barricaded city,

smoke rising from the burning buildings,
the Algonquin's ashes,
Dorothy Parker's derrière.

Just then the phone rang
like a ghost of sound
and Robinson pulled the cord from the wall.

In the rooftops he could see
how easy it would be
to fly too close to the sun

but Robinson thought better of it
and sat down on the bed
as Ann breathed air from who knows where.

April 21, 2006

SUNDAY AT FIVE

"Hello. Yes, this is Robinson. Sunday
at five? I'd love to. Pretty well. And you?"
As he hung up he knew he didn't mean it.

He thought of his affair with Mrs. Morse,
those stretch marks on her belly,
the cellulite on the back of her thighs,

the vast star-field in her eyes,
the air almost visible
swirling about in the room,

clinging to sheets, to curtains, to lungs.
Sunday at five, what was Robinson thinking?
He put his hand through his black hair

as if that would solve the problem.
"The city is tyrannosaurus rexes," he thought
"that eat men

in the subway, in plain view on the streets,
even in front of the police station."
Robinson would not look at Robinson in the mirror.

April 22, 2006

HOUSE OF ROBINSON

Mrs. Morse took a bath
after making love with Robinson
for the second time this week.

Earlier on the way to Robinson's gray apartment
her heart beat like a cop's nightstick
against a skull.

Since there was no answer
when she rang the doorbell,
she took out the key

Robinson had given her and let herself in.
He arrived much later
with justifiable stories about a poet he knew.

In his arms she made nonverbal noises.
Robinson was always quiet,
barely uttering a sound during nirvana.

She peered into his soul
like one would look into an abandoned house,
but the house made her look away.

April 22, 2006

ROBINSON'S LIBRARY

God is seen looking around for God,
the beach bereft of water,
wind so strong it bends itself.

Robinson is back at Berkeley
arranging his library
around Ann's thighs,

her ankles a volcano.
But the thoughts of this moment
might as well be covered in snow

because, unfortunately, the smiles of the bathers
have followed Robinson home
dragging high-tide to the door.

April 22, 2006

KING KONG

"I wonder if it's lonely being King Kong?"
Robinson wonders as he falls
from the top of the Empire State Building

down to the hard concrete
that wakes him up from his dream.
He goes right back to sleep.
The carpet gathers itself on the floor
woven by machines
sweated over by the working class,

the metal frame of the bed
put together in a dirty shop
by rough, callused hands

which don't pick up the *New York Times*
or use the *Tribune*
only to patch a broken windowpane.

The cannery workers
who put the canned food in his pantry
would ignore poetry unless it gave them a raise.

April 23, 2006

THE SOUND OF ICE CUBES

When other people talked of joy or happiness,
Robinson looked away
and banished such foolishness.

The elevated train went by,
its noise made of rusted metal
that never needs feelings.

The buildings stand tall and proud,
they glance at the sea
because all they can do is glance.

Robinson took a drink
that would lead to another drink
until he was drunk.

"Happiness is admiring elephants in the park,
the sound of ice cubes dropped in a glass."
He read Toynbee backwards.

Devoid of highs and lows
would be fine he thought
before he sank into a chair in darkness.

April 24, 2006

ON THE BEACH

Robinson in flowered trunks,
eyes toward the breakers.
"What was it Matthew Arnold said

about the ebb and flow…?"
Robinson couldn't recall at the moment.
How long had the sea

been making this sound?
How long can it keep
making this sound?

He felt the sea between his toes,
the broken shell of a sea creature
shattered who knows when?

What kind of life
had that sea creature lived?
A life like Robinson's?

He flung his cigarette butt into the surf,
a jellyfish rang twice clear as a bell
and was gone.

April 24, 2006

RELEGATED TO ROBINSON

Somewhere in Brooklyn, early fall,
the leaves dive-bomb like kamikaze Orientals
in the sky above Manhattan,

the smoke rising from factories
where human beings are slaves to themselves,
gladiators with no coliseum,

not torn apart by lions
but by the very labor which pays their way.
The sewing machines rape women.

Robinson walks by garbage men
battling an army of trash.
The city issues them no medals.

Yet, Robinson sees nothing but himself,
the streets, the noise, thousands of people
along his way do not exist.

April 24, 2006

EAST SIDE BARS

When the night ends Robinson finds Robinson
in East Side bars,
he drinks a part of himself with each drink,

he shuns the bar mirror.
He does not look at the bartender,
the bartender always knows what Robinson needs.

Occasionally Robinson glances over
at the figure of a woman,
her skirt is ankle-length,

a hat covers her head,
the flamingo pin on her lapel
far away as Africa to him.

The barstool creaks
as Robinson turns around.
His watch is ticking a sound he does not hear.

A sound like a stampede of buffaloes
in the American West
and Indians shot dead

by Robinson's fellow man
just a few short decades ago — not that Robinson cares.
He swallows the icy drink with his heart.

April 25, 2006

THE MISSING LINKS

The Algonquin rises like the sun,
the missing links parade in and out.
Prufrock, in an overcoat,

thinking he's still in England
nods to Robinson a greeting
Robinson doesn't seem to acknowledge.

Pigeons fly overhead retaining history
as part of a newspaper flies down the street,
the pigeons questioning, "what kind of bird is that?"

Robinson is meeting friends for coffee.
They talk about a song he's composed,
a friend admires his Glen plaid jacket

but Robinson's mind soars a million miles away,
a pterodactyl and the world viewed
with pterodactyl eyes.

April 25, 2006

NATURAL BLOOM CIGARS

Under a sign for Natural Bloom Cigars
a girl tugs at her underclothes as she walks.
Robinson cannot help but notice.

He records it in his mind —
the shape of her hips,
the sway nature has over nature,

the animal instinct to pounce,
to ravish, to cast asunder.
Let the hyenas have the rest.

Her high heels click on the pavement
like a mouse would click
years hence on a Word document.

A word that escapes Robinson right now,
the flesh, after all,
is not meant for words.

April 25, 2006

SUMMERS ON THE CAPE

Robinson was out of town,
spending the summer on the Cape,
strolling on the beach

he denied eye contact even to the gulls,
a sandcastle of some skill
caught his attention,

he contemplated flotsam and jetsam,
the greatness of the sea,
the sea uncaring—

justified in Robinson's mind.
As a group of bathers walked towards him
he aimed for the dunes,

the sound of the surf changed,
he tried to decipher the new meaning
as the wind poured through the sand.

April 25, 2006

PLASTIC VENUS

Robinson stopped and gazed into a window
where a plastic Venus, modeling a truss,
looked out at Robinson,

her missing arm roaming the ancient world,
lying somewhere still intact,
reaching across time

and time swatting it away.
The things men are capable of
bound only by imagination.

The picture-window into our souls
made of unbreakable glass,
a door allows you in but not out.

Robinson thought he saw his own head
shaped like the Sphinx
reflected on the window for a split second.

He thought about it for awhile
as the desert unfolded before him
but he fought off the sand and heat,

the perspiration cooled his body,
the street became wide again
and his lungs grew back.

April 25, 2006

THE ROOMS OF ROBINSON

The rooms of Robinson have no walls,
windows will not close,
doors will not budge shut,

the blinking sign outside
advertising rum or corsets
is blinding on the floor next to his bed.

Robinson kicks it, gives up,
covers his head with a pillow
and tries to go to sleep.

The dreams come back
like Cardinals in the Vatican
dead before they become Pope,

Italians sifted like flour,
traffic re-routed around Robinson
as he pulls on the sheets.

The park trees, though they are blocks away,
want to show Robinson their rings.
A neighbor makes granite noise in the hall

before he gets into the elevator.
"At this time of the night!"
Robinson cursed.

His words bounced along the floor,
snagged on the carpet
and stood there astonished.

April 25, 2006

ROBINSON'S HIGH NOON DREAM

Delmore hated Robinson
and would go out of his way
to diminish Robinson's gifts,

the vast city was not big enough
for the both of them,
word-slingers, one dressed in white,

one dressed in black
(this would be Robinson, of course)
the sun in Robinson's eyes

as Delmore drew first, fired
and in a stupor missed,
crumpled to Times Square filth like a big bear.

Robinson did not shoot,
looked at the skyline,
walked uptown like Gary Cooper,

put his hands in his pocket,
forgot the incident
like childhood memories of sadness.

To the townspeople
the woman and the buckboard
did not seem reward enough.

Robinson sneered on his way out of Dodge,
the mountains in the distance
made of dust.

April 25, 2006

LATE FOR A MOVIE

The Hudson wears its dirty topcoat,
a gold watch would not spruce it up.
There's a Bogie movie in town

Robinson wants to catch.
When he gets home his wife is pulling nylons
over her thighs,

a surge of desire rushes
through his body and passes.
He sits down pensively

in his own darkening,
he tries to shock himself
but electricity has never been invented.

Nobody thought of fire or wheels.
"Aren't we going to be late
for the movie?" says his wife.

He looks at her as if she were
some strange prehistoric creature
like himself.

He helps her with her coat,
they go out and he locks the door
with a stone.

April 25, 2006

THE AFRICAN QUEEN

Robinson comes out of the theater
holding his wife by the waist,
the crowd chatters about *The African Queen*.

At the coffee shop Robinson does not listen
to the conversation between himself
and his wife,

she's talking about the African romance.
Robinson could imagine
the spinster naked,

elbow bones here, bony knees
tossed in the air,
the river noises hiding her sighs

but then he drifted off to melancholy.
Some epic he would write
about something specifically unimportant.

"Why are you putting so much sugar
in your coffee?" says his wife.
He thinks out loud, "Trying to sweeten Lake Victoria."

"Oh, honey," she confesses,
"I wish I was where you are."
But Robinson was somewhere else by then.

April 26, 2006

SUBWAY HOME

On the subway home
his wife was in a good mood,
making hippo-ear imitations

like Charlie and Rosie
while Robinson could only muster up
an image of the African soldiers

shooting at the boat in the bend of the river.
No one could see steam venting from Robinson
as he propelled himself down the rapids,

rocks protruding, white-water menacing,
boat jumping in the air
as if to get away,

there is no getting free he told the boat.
Robinson knew all the nooks and crannies
of disappointment,

the darkness pouring into the sun
and the sun being unable
to put up a fight.

April 26, 2006

A DARK SNOW

All winter long, it seemed,
a dark snow had kept falling,
snowflake stabbing snowflake

in the muddy ditch
outside of Robinson's apartment.
The sludge resembled snowmen gone bad.

Christmas lights on Broadway
were colorless reflected in his eyes
even though Robinson kept his head down,

his fedora pointing at the horizon.
The shoppers appeared confident
in Macys or Shorty's Liquor Store,

whiskey looking out at the city,
rum running out of patience,
God a percent of alcohol.

Robinson bought his bottle
and hurriedly smoked a cigarette
that burned the city down to his fingers.

April 26, 2006

THE HANGING

With a noose around his neck
and the captain of the Louisa
giving orders for them to hang Robinson,

Allnut's homemade torpedoes go off
sinking the ship almost immediately
and Robinson is saved once again.

Robinson does not fight it—
when you're in the middle of a lake
you have to swim ashore,

when you're on top of Kilimanjaro
surrounded by a glacier
you're going to have to find the way down,

the forest at the foothills full of predatory animals
waiting to tear Robinson apart
like the naked jungle of New York City,

the rope-burn on his neck proves it.
The phone rings somewhere in the room
and scatters wildebeest.

April 27, 2006

MORNING COFFEE

Once ashore, Robinson wakes up in bed,
his wife's hand on his shoulder,
he slides out of bed to make coffee,

the traffic outside is making the noise
all traffic has memorized,
violent buildings hold it all in,

immigrant faces look strange in sugar
as Robinson looks out
the second-story window.

Buses transport worker ants
down into holes
to save the queen,

the subway's full of termites
white from not having seen the sun
that rotates around earth.

Robinson put bread into the toaster
until the toast popped up
in his mind.

Robinson did not hear the sounds
his wife made in the toilet
or hear her wash her hands and face.

He did not see her brush her hair
in the mirror Robinson used only
as certain demarcation.

April 27, 2006

A RACE LIKE ROBINSON

Robinson was in Washington D.C.
when he heard the news like everybody else
that a visitor from another world had landed

and caused havoc throughout the city,
the country, throughout the world
by merely turning off the electricity.

Robinson laughed until he heard
that the visitor and his giant robot
had destroyed an entire Army

and then he wondered if there were
Robinsons on this other world,
strolling about under umbrellas,

shuffling their feet at a bakery,
sea-sick on an escalator?
He went to see the spaceship.

The robot was motionless
until it sensed Robinson was near
and it opened it's faceplate to look at Robinson,

almost as if he perceived a brother.
After a moment it closed its eyes,
Robinson buried a cigarette-butt in the grass with his foot.

April 28, 2006

MILK BOWL

The world can drive us crazy
even if we're already crazy
thought Robinson as he opened his mail,

a letter from Randall Jarrell
praised this line or that.
A note from Rexroth about Tu Fu.

Robinson poured a bowl of milk for the cat,
the cat meowed, licked
and came up with a milk-mustache,

groomed its fur, meowed again,
rubbed up against Robinson's leg,
disappeared around the corner.

Robinson had forgotten what he was thinking
and turned his attention
to the mail again after he picked up the bowl

from the surface of the floor.
He rinsed the bowl out in the sink,
the clockwise maelstrom disappeared

down to the depths of the city
to be received by the East River
as close to a blessing as any river could hope for,

the returning of water
so it could be returned to the sea
and from the sea returned to the sky and back again.

Oddly, Robinson looked up at a primordial sea
at the creatures around him.
He swam in unison with the school.

April 28, 2006

HARMONIUM

Robinson poured over Wallace Stevens,
the poetry was not as dull
as the man,

the boring man sitting on the couch
thinking about the odds,
listening to the radio,

reading the *Wall Street Journal*,
his reading-glasses
sticking to his face like a frown.

Is the poetry at home in the city,
Bronx, Brooklyn, Harlem?
Let's not judge

thought Robinson as he closed *Harmonium*.
This man is much like myself thought Robinson
as he flew across town like Superman,

the kryptonite was himself,
green, full of the taste
he dreaded as a child and now.

April 28, 2006

THE CONQUERING HERO

Robinson roamed the lush jungles of Mexico,
the Sonoran desert, the Vera Cruz beaches,
the contested Indian lands,

he climbed the pyramids with Malcolm Lowry,
he partook of La Malinche
because that's what white men do

he thought as he looked into the mirror to shave,
being careful not to make eye contact,
being careful not to look into his soul by accident.

He dried his face with a towel.
He looked out his hotel window,
was that El Popo smoking

or was that the whole of Mexico blowing up?
Robinson packed his suitcase,
went downstairs quietly, a sad Conquistador.

May 1, 2006

LÁZARO CÁRDENAS

Years later President Cárdenas promised
to bring democracy to Mexico
but it didn't quite work out that way

thought Robinson as he looked at Denver down below,
the mountains full of snow,
the road almost empty,

skyline as unimpressive as living there,
clean air its only gift.
Robinson sitting in a diner

hundreds of miles from Mexico,
appreciative of it, but disillusioned.
Back home a clay Mayan head

sat on his desk across the ages
and in the jungle of his mind.
Robinson climbs the steep steps of a pyramid,

one wrong step, sacrificial,
one wrong step, a plunge to death
thought Robinson as he steadied himself.

Just then Robinson noticed an old Mayan looking at him,
he seemed to be amused by Robinson's plight
and unconcerned by the decimation of the Maya.

Robinson put a spoon in his soup,
put more sugar in his tea.
The street dragged a pedestrian past the window.

May 1, 2006

PARKING LOT

Robinson parked his Plymouth,
the dirty salt air hit his face,
he felt like slapping it back,

the bridge rose like a behemoth,
like something Ahab would battle,
something that would subdue Job once and for all,

something to entangle clouds or wind.
Robinson walked up the path
with the earth beneath him all the way to China

and then the precipice of the Chinese sky,
a Chinaman speaking Mandarin Robinson joked
as he walked into the grass,

its leaves like daggers in his heart.
He touched his chest
but there was no blood,

individual atoms fell out of the wind
and bounced along on the ground.
An electron startled Robinson.

May 2, 2006

NEVER CHANGED A FLAT

Robinson never put water in the radiator,
he never changed the oil,
he never changed a flat or windshield wiper.

In that, he was like most of you.
He never squealed his tires
or drove too fast,

he gripped the steering wheel
at nine and three,
he avoided heavy traffic.

Robinson ignored machines
as much as he could,
his thoughts cut in half by music.

He wrote the words down,
stood back, got closer in,
was happy with the tune,

until his thoughts drifted towards him.
He did not relish being himself
as he slammed the car door,

not that he was angry at the piece of metal,
no, it just didn't close right
unless you really gave it a good shove.

He walked his Robinson gait
upon the faded asphalt
which had grown between the trees of time.

May 3, 2006

PART TWO

THE AFTERIMAGES

TRASH IN THE STREETS

The trash in the street gathers itself
being put to shame by man's indifference.
Robinson doesn't seem to notice,

he wraps the coat around himself
in the chill of fall.
Roman leather would not do

against this enemy.
The lions of Robinson's coliseum
growl and circle,

once indoor they are subdued
by Robinson's puffing on panatelas.
Smoke curls angry

even though the long nails
only scratch the surface.
The lions and Robinson have become one.

THE BIRDS

The birds circle in the skyscrapers.
In the kitchenette Robinson prepares
pancakes in the image of man,

his black ribs still covered in sand.
A phone rings in the living room
but it resonates in the sky,

its sound visible and ignored,
wires shoot straight up a thousand feet
tinted by the wind.

Robinson finally answers.
He's to review a book of poems
by a sad poet.

His coffee tastes like a rug,
pancakes float in front of his chair.
He looks at the spoon as if it's become a wall.

The birds circle in the skyscrapers
but do not land, do not focus, do not glide,
trapped, as they are, in Robinson's mind.

WELCOME TO TODAY

The radio shakes like an atomic bomb,
Robinson wakes up with a start.
For a moment he doesn't know

if it's his wife next to him
or his mistress Mrs. Morse
(and does it really matter?)

Of course not, he tells himself,
once he comes to his senses.
They fit in their underwear different

he begins to think before his mind hurries
to whatever the day may hold.
He flushes the toilet,

the water becomes clear again.
The ocean pours back into the tank,
killer whales, sharks, manta rays

swim in panic and confusion.
Welcome to the club
Robinson motions, aware but uncaring.

MONKEY MAN

Robinson meets friends at a bar,
the human glasses fill with human blood,
but everyone laughs and jokes.

Robinson surprises himself by laughing, too.
What ghost has been shaken loose,
what fire escape has not rusted in Harlem,

what airplane has damaged the sky
beyond repair, how will we fly again?
Has anyone bothered to tell the birds?

They say goodnight, head in different directions.
The subway rattles, turns, stops,
rattles on again like evolution.

Robinson is hanging from trees,
his prehensile tail does him no good.
He flings excrement at New Yorkers.

When he gets to his apartment
Ann is asleep, cold supper on the table.
Cold food doesn't hinder polar bears.

From one chunk of ice to another,
and black and white dreams of continental drift
Robinson finally falls asleep.

FOUL BALL

The peanut-munching crowd
gathers to praise triumphant Robinson.
The foul ball nearby

bounces with a thud
and ends up in some bruiser's glove,
the brute hands the ball lovingly to his son.

Robinson's been persuaded
to attend the game
by Mrs. Morse, damn Yankee fans,

their pinstripes settle against the centerfielder.
Robinson's thoughts migrate
to Mrs. Morse,

the mole above her knee, hidden by her skirt,
fine, invisible velvet hair.
A fast ball in the catcher's mitt

echoes in the shortcomings of right field.
Robinson strikes out, throws his bat
at the opposing team's dugout.

The boos follow him all the way home.
Only the filth of the city
cheers him as he climbs the steps.

THE BULLFIGHT

Why did he let her talk him into going
to the baseball game,
the beasts of his human race

always wear him out,
their flesh exposed to the elements,
the elements themselves exposed, gaunt

ferris wheel proud of its staggering height.
Magellan proved the world
was only half round

and Robinson still believes it so.
Like a Spaniard
he will persist living in caves, he insists

that bullfights deserve more credit than baseball,
there is no deception,
the pure joy of killing for pleasure,

the crowds forgiven by the Pope.
Robinson has no such recourse
so he suffers in hallways, kitchens, bedrooms.

THE PERPETRATOR

He reviews the book by the sad poet.
The faun in love with
an 18th century poetess,

petticoat layer after petticoat layer
in her everyday life,
her rebellion against men.

And this frail man praises her.
Robinson will not persecute him,
he's too exhausted for that.

The city thunders outside,
the sun wears on him,
taxis sweat yellow,

the taxi drivers stink of police barricades.
Who's been murdered, maimed, or raped
this time?

The perpetrator flees through Robinson,
destroying internal organs as he runs,
the curtains should have kept him out.

FIGHTING THE PIGEONS

Ground-dragging skies keep pigeons
from roosting in our souls,
soiling God's gift,

instead they roost at obtuse angles.
Robinson swings his sword at them,
feathers flying, the pigeons

slam their brakes, screech to a halt.
What's this madman doing,
their birdbrains ask?

They fly to the Empire State Building,
to the Chrysler Building,
certainly Central Park isn't safe, they wonder?

Robinson puts his sword away,
walks to the lake, takes out his sword again
and cuts the lake in half.

"Robinson, how does that make you feel?"
He hears an echo in his head
of empty Manhattan.

The iron beams of the buildings are exposed,
the brick and cement are gone
from Robinson's heart.

It does not matter if the streets
have a home or not,
he convinces himself and a startled bystander.

Slowly the pigeons return
and co-exist with Robinson
on the sharp edge of the island.

Robinson buttons his shirt,
looks in the mirror at his dark mustache,
runs thumb and index finger over it.

FIRE ISLAND

He goes away on vacation,
a two day getaway to Fire Island,
the wheels of the Atlantic roll ashore,

brake wet with sea, salt-corroding sky,
children and parents
unaware great fish veer at them,

lost ships foam, missing Navy planes surface,
the tin can of Atlantis
is being kicked by teenagers into the dunes.

On the horizon a freighter
hurries to deliver goods that support
the bad as well as the god-fearing.

Robinson grabs his towel,
wipes off the sand
created by Poseidon a zillion years ago.

The ebb and flow bewilders Robinson
so he heads back to his cabin.
Ann squirms like mermaids in seaweed nests.

These vacations seem to wear him out,
do more harm than good
and leave him out of touch with his unease.

ARRIVAL OF ROBINSON

It comes as a surprise to Ann
when Robinson tells her to pack the bags
for an extended trip to Mexico,

she wonders what to wear to a volcano
and Robinson shakes his head.
Pack shorts to climb the pyramids,

learn Spanish to talk to the natives.
Grand races used to occupy the land
but now it's ravished by the peasantry,

they drive cars like burros,
they marry their daughters off at twelve.
The sun burns a hole in their heads, he's sure.

Ann questioned Robinson but Robinson
was busy trying to calm
the viciousness of his conquistador.

The spears bounced off of him,
the arrows, the rocks, the whole war party.
Robinson, the disgusted conquering hero

to his own spleen, to his own horses.
He pulls one stone from the pyramid
and the whole thing comes tumbling down.

AZTEC DEFEAT

Bruised and battered, mad-hattered,
they reach Acapulco
still smelling of Aztec stone,

the smell of Aztec defeat prevalent.
They want to shed their skin,
lips of the feathered serpent

like lipstick in Ann's compact mirror.
Robinson's hands are purple
until he hangs up the purple towel.

They get in their bathing suits,
a demeanor of the beach
is all Robinson can promulgate,

a Mexican girl brings the drinks.
The sand between his toes
struggles as he crushes it,

soon a fine dust floats above them,
surf echoes, then eliminates
all other sound

except the sound of Robinson's heartbeat.
Sea creatures swim as far away
as natural laws allow,

come full circle to Vera Cruz
and Robinson's pounding blood
spurts through their bodies still.

Robinson and Ann
retire to their cabin.
She turns the lights off in his chest.

GOLDEN GATE

They fly from Acapulco to San Francisco
where Robinson has thoughts of relocating.
The Golden Gate Bridge comes into view,

the sea in his eyes, white-caps break like glass
against his jacket sleeves
as he moves his arm onto the armrest.

Ann sleeps, the clouds fly.
Someone's intentions worked out well,
he thinks. The airplane window so thick

it would take eons to drill through it,
but Robinson doesn't have the time
and turns back to the sacrilegious present.

He wakes Ann; they're on the glide path,
the city rises up to meet them
like the family dog.

The cold nose of San Francisco
seems to agree with Robinson,
it brings out the terror in him,

the terror he needs and cherishes.
The cable cars tear into his flesh,
that's ok, that's alright, fine, he whispers.

BRIDGING THE GAP

They drive across the bridge,
pity the poor souls who labored up here
to create this monstrosity and marvel

thought Robinson when they reached the other side.
They turned right back around.
Puffing on his cigar

as they strolled Fisherman's Wharf,
devoured seafood like coastal people,
fish eating fish, ambushing,

disguised as sand, as stone, as anemone.
They swallowed everything headfirst,
the snake had taught Eve that much.

Soon they must fly back to New York,
Robinson's stomach would be in a knot
to get back home,

his sweaty palms would never dry,
the biblical flood of sweat, pillars of salt.
Robinson's soul dies of thirst.

NEW YORK, NEW YORK

Sometimes the blood demands blood.
Back in New York
Robinson relishes the affront of the city,

the nastiness, the ogre of mankind,
God forbid this traffic was dinosaurs,
stegosaurus, brontosaurus, T-rex,

the sharp teeth of buildings,
blood-thirsty Macy's coming straight at you
before it dismembers shoppers instead.

Robinson continues on to the Village,
he's looking for a particular book
to cross check a review.

He ponders the silly poet holed up
in some flea-bag hotel,
writing epics, surrounded by giant rats.

Robinson kicks them away,
but they come right back, endearing.
How can man live this way? he yells!

He buys the book he needs,
he heads back toward the vast
and empty halls of poetry,

unending warehouse filled
with abandoned creations.
What fools! He feels the statement

attack his chest, cobwebs shake
with freshly trapped insects in his mind.
They do not taste that bad.

A snide smile spreads across his face.
The juice, the crunchiness
of the human race finally surfaces.

He slams the warehouse door shut.
From the outside it looks so nondescript,
rusted tin, wind blown trash all about,

derelicts, dirty and smelling of cheap wine
ask Robinson for a spare dime.
Robinson has outworn his welcome with himself.

RENDEZVOUS

Robinson called on Mrs. Morse.
It had been almost a month and a half
since their last meeting.

She had told him over the phone
that Mr. Morse would be away on business
for the next two days.

When Robinson arrived at her apartment,
she was wearing an Ionian nightgown,
satin, sheer, as he followed her

to the bedroom he was hypnotized
by the undulations.
Had it been this way for Adam,

the sudden rabid desire,
attacking in pairs of arms and legs,
hair, sinew, cluttered savanna of the mind.

Sitting up in bed he sees
the hyenas approaching for their share.
He promises to call her tomorrow.

LADY LIBERTY

Feeling guilty over the forbidden things
Mrs. Morse endures with zest,
he calls her up early,

"I thought I'd take you
to the Statue of Liberty today,
and lunch afterwards."

She's excited as she puts down the receiver,
starts going through the closet
for just the right outfit.

They climb to the top of the Statue,
look back at the skyline
where monsters, men and mice

eke out a living one way or another.
He holds her by the waist,
lust surges below the surface,

flies underwater to Staten Island and back,
just to prove it can be done.
The hourglass sand pours through Robinson.

AT HURLEY'S

He took her to Hurley's for lunch,
climbing the stairs to the third floor.
Robinson made sure he didn't run into pigeons,

clouds, anything headed
to La Guardia, a stray Nazi blimp,
anything disagreeable.

The waiter seats them by a window.
She orders seafood from the cold ocean,
creatures choking in nets,

a Frankenstein crew pulls them on board,
the Gulf Stream continues empty to Britain.
Robinson orders a steak.

In New Jersey an Italian caveman
splits a cow's head in half with a dull axe,
the cow stands there, not registering the event.

They enjoy their meal.
Outside the window, down there,
pedestrian ants pursue their nonsense,

different from Robinson and his mistress
only by the luck of antennae.
The tip on the table tolerates gravity.

He kisses her on the sidewalk, looks around
to make sure all these strangers
are indeed strangers like him.

Yes, yes, he doesn't know himself,
yes, yes, he doesn't know her as well
as he knows her body and his.

WITNESS FOR THE PERSECUTION

Ann has suspected as much,
that hint of strange perfume.
Sometimes she lies in bed,

she touches him, she reaches for him
and he just lies there
like the sheets, like cold weather,

like ice on ice, she caresses
the iceberg, it doesn't melt.
She finally turns over and goes to sleep.

But today she had followed him,
watched him and the woman board the ferry,
waited the hours for them to return,

followed them to the restaurant,
loitered on the sidewalk across the street,
hidden by strangers,

watched him kiss her on the mouth.
Kiss her on the cheek, let her be your friend,
kiss her on the cheek, she screamed

inside herself, but no, he held the woman
by the waist in an all too familiar way.
Tears poured down Ann's cheeks,

nobody looked at her face, nobody cared,
nobody gave a damn.
She took the subway home to hell.

THE FIGHT

As she opened the door
she heard him in the kitchen,
she doesn't want to go in there,

but as soon as she's facing him,
he knows it and looks down at his shoes.
"Who is that woman, is she your whore,

is she your slut, I saw you kiss her
on the mouth, you can't tell me
she's just a friend!"

He tries to say something.
She throws a cup at him,
it bounces off his shoulder,

the shrapnel pierces his heart,
he falls on the cup
as it spins on the floor.

He falls on the cup
as if he was a soldier
sacrificing himself by falling on a grenade

to save his buddies.
In Flanders Field the poppies grow
so far away and yet so very near.

THE RECONCILIATION

The reconciliation took time,
even God was called in to build
earthen dams, to re-route streets,

to battle city hall and its red tape,
to negotiate with La Cosa Nostra,
to bugger teamsters, crooked cops and preachers.

God took the East River over one shoulder,
the Hudson over the other shoulder
and siphoned rubbish, fish, footballs,

glass, old rusted cars, six days
turned into months and finally Robinson
was allowed back into his own apartment.

It would be longer before
they became man and wife.
A few trash cans still stumbled in their blood.

The lids separated from the cans,
from the trash, from the smells.
Robinson made a tin can sound as he kissed her.

She recoiled but then acquiesced.
Soon Robinson was himself again,
morose, matching gray wall against gray wall.

They walked outside to the busy street,
tried to subtract every one, children, cops, taxis.
The wind twisting in their fingers.

Time works its magic
by finding your card every time,
in piles of marbles, manatees or mountains.

Its marauders leave the land glistening.
If you look at Robinson he blinds you,
slabs of him, chunks of him roll uphill.

Robinson offers one of his rare smiles as he and Ann
force themselves through the maddening crowds
which crawl on all four out of buildings.

THE MAP OF LIFE

Robinson could see the rebar in the clouds,
bent out of shape, rusted,
ready to stab, infect, or just ignore you.

The rain rained upon itself.
The huge desert city down below
expected and received nothing,

an occasional shadow or two
drifted overhead,
and the rain dropped its pretense.

The subway passengers were gray,
or black & white if they stood on the *New York Herald*.
The hand-holds shoved greasy histories at you,

not at anybody else, only at you.
Robinson dug in his heels,
until he got to his apartment,

pulled back the curtains
to see where he had been,
to know where he was going.

March 12, 2007

THE NAKED CITY

The trees are bare, the birds are bare
in Robinson's chest and shoulders,
the branches rattle as they climb down.

Every building in New York City,
in the Bronx, in Brooklyn, in Queens
has lost its windows,

has lost its doors, even the tallest buildings
sport a single floor,
the echoes are horrendous,

and reverberate out into the Atlantic,
up the Hudson River.
Robinson meets friends for a drink,

they've lost their faces.
No arms, no legs, just torsos,
yet everybody's cheerful, jolly, jubilant.

On the street, the cars have been turned inside out,
the steering wheels, the seats, the drivers,
the blaring radios are bolted to the outside.

The tires do not seem out of place
piled inside next to bumpers,
trunk, hood, and windshield wipers.

Robinson nods goodbye to his friends,
walks down the street
towards the cemented sky forever.

March 11, 2007

THE COLLECTED POEMS OF ARTEMIO SÁNCHEZ

2009

STARTING OVER

Artemio Sánchez returns to his hometown
thirty years after having moved to Minnesota.
Hell, his frozen neighbor is the Hispanic
poet Ray González.

Lupita left La Rata and moved to Houston,
Meme married a divorcee from Nuquis,
El Caballo still works at the chicken plant.

They say El Beatle moved somewhere up north
and became a writer
but, no one knows for sure.

Speedy never made it back from Viet Nam,
La Reina del Diez y Seis at Hidalgo Hall
died of cancer last year—

so many putos had the hots for her back then.
But when you visit the old hometown now
only strange Mexicans stare at you from Seguin.

It's no longer nomás Yogi Berra's déjà vu.
You've become a stranger
in your own land once again!

March 3, 2007

IN THE TUBERCULAR HOSPITAL

Pancho López, owner of Hidalgo Hall,
couldn't take it and fled
the tubercular hospital before he was cured.

Mr. García collapsed in the hallway.
Artemio was ten feet behind him
when his old, bald head hit the floor.

The orderlies carried him to his cubicle dead.
Gil came from legendary Rosenberg cotton
to fall in love with Nancy the nurse.

Rod, the male orderly, talked like a girl.
Margaret the lunch lady
made wonderful, runny eggs.

Artemio wrote poetry to pass the day,
Artemio wrote poetry to pass the night
until Dr. Frankenstein cut out Artemio's lungs.

April 1, 2007

ARTEMIO SÁNCHEZ EL QUINCEAÑERO

Back in 1963 when Artemio was fifteen
he spent a year and a half
in the San Antonio tubercular hospital.

The hospital was divided into wings,
you know, like schools.
All males in one wing,

all females in another.
One day Artemio noticed
a new arrival in the women's section,

a girl named La Margaret
from San Marcos,
home of poeta Villanueva.

Artemio courted La Margaret,
unsuccessfully, until two months later
when her sister Dominga arrived.

A lot of Mexicans got TB back then.
Anyway, Artemio and Minga became an item,
and exchanged bacilli with their besos.

April 1, 2007

ARTEMIO'S VENGEANCE

Artemio grew his own lungs
like a lizard Quetzalcoatl
grows back his severed tail.

Artemio tasted the new air
silent upon a peak like Balboso
in Highland Hills.

Artemio toured the Mission San José
when Spanish priests
enslaved and brain-washed Indians.

Artemio heard Kennedy speak
across the street
from the tubercular hospital.

Kennedy was offering a New Frontier,
apparently there were other lands
to be stolen from the Moon Mexicans.

April 2, 2007

ARTEMIO SÁNCHEZ TODAY

Kennedy was shot the next day in Dallas,
Artemio watched the black & white broadcasts
on the hospital television

along with the other "inmates."
Artemio often wondered about
this other country

which existed alongside his,
occasionally bleeding over
into his own Mexican world.

The other Mexicans across the border
were completely unknown to him.
His great-grandparents

had been born in Tejas.
He was confused
not only about the meaning of his life,

but also about the mixed-up world
that preached one thing
and practiced another.

So Artemio decided to keep the identity
he kept inside his own head,
and to this day he honors it,

and, of course, he pays the price for it,
but, at least, he doesn't have to pay for it
in dollars.

April 2, 2007

VÁMONOS PORQUE AQUÍ ASUSTAN

Artemio had made that
fateful trip back to Seguin,
and it's true what they say,

the more things change
the more they stay the same.
At fifty-nine,

Artemio is still the same child of ten
holding his grandfather's hand
in Normanna, Texas

where the gringo tells his grandfather,
"We don't serve Mexicans here!"
so they drove on down the road

to buy hamburgers in another dusty town
where other gringos did serve Mexicans.
Now, as Artemio drives to Corpus Christi

to partake of the beaches,
he drives through the ghost town
which used to be Normanna.

April 3, 2007

ARTEMIO, THE TOWELED-SERPENT

God, look at Artemio's skinny legs
as he strolls on the sand
of this misnamed Padre Island.

The bikinied girls show off
their cubistic pubistic,
but Artemio turns around

as they walk by
because he's an ass man.
The offshore oil wells

litter the gulf within sight
of Artemio's hotel.
The freighters appear glued

to the horizon,
the seagulls swarm
over children who toss bread

into the clear blue sky.
For the moment, Artemio
has lost the whole of Aztlan.

He's not even a Chicano right now,
he's barely human,
towel in hand, sand between his toes,

sunglasses hiding his eyes.
The waves arrive and arrive,
and for a million years

having been looking for Artemio,
but by now
he's on the fourth floor balcony

of his hotel, out of reach,
out of sight.
The waves, bewildered, turn back.

April 5, 2007

NAMESAKE

Artemio was not named
after the Greek god Artemus,
he was not named

after Artemis Gordon
of *The Wild, Wild West* TV show sidekick
(that would be anachronistic, anyway)

no, he was not named
after his great-grandfather
Artemio Gerónimo Sánchez

who is best remembered
in family history
because he is known to

have killed Indians and white men
in his heyday.
The modern day Artemio

tries to use his poetry
as his hatchet
to carry out his hatchet jobs.

April 7, 2007

RANDOM THOUGHTS ON THE WAY
TO HIS HOTEL

Artemio gets into the green & white taxi
with the word written
in Mexican Black Letter.

In the distance a pyramid
to get rid of, he thinks.
Old Spanish guts still spilled, there, he points.

Paz said La Malinche did it for moola
with a mula, it's difficult
to assess the difficulty therein.

The better part of the Aztec race
joined the other side
claims the same Paz

and the cowardly lion Efraín Huerta
was afraid of the delicious door,
he called it, la puerta rica.

Artemio finally arrives at his hotel,
The Hotel Moctezuma,
the pick pocket

eight year old boys
swirl like Tasmanian devils
in the nearby alley.

April 23, 2007

THE CLIMBER OF HEIGHTS

Artemio climbs the Pyramid of the Sun,
not to pay homage to his ancestors.
No, indeed, because Artemio's ancestors

were dirty Indians from
modern day Tamaulipas,
living off fish and flotsam,

content with fish-eye soup,
mounting their women doggy-style,
greasing their hair with animal fat.

Whatever past he has, he's proud of it.
Artemio's never been a denier.
He's an honorable fellow, not Spanish at all.

April 25, 2007

OBSERVATIONS OFF THE TOP OF HIS HEAD

The view from the top is majestic,
the poverty polite,
the sun a little older than in olden times.

Artemio swallows,
takes a deep breath,
starts down at an obscene angle.

What were these brown bastards thinking,
couldn't they be satisfied
with climbing volcanoes?

What kind of knuckleheads
would amputate the heart,
hold it up high for praise?

Not that it would save their asses —
though millions of them have survived.
"I repeat, not that it would save their asses."

April 25, 2007

FLYING MEXICANA

At the conference, Artemio tries to explain
how he, as a poet, got to this point
in his creative career.

He goes back to his roots,
the Olmec head of his great-grandfather,
a lowly go-fer no doubt.

And how Artemio groveled his way up
from nothing in the white man's eyes,
to nothing in his own brown community.

"So it is this art I am obligated to..."
he curses and smiles.
"It's our humor that brings us tears," he promises.

Outside, you can wrap the smog in tamales,
eat the corn leaves, down cervezas,
eye the behinds of women.

A slight earthquake is not enough
to shake up Artemio.
He's due to fly back to clueless America tonight.

To be welcomed by the skyline
of ice-cream cone buildings
cold as Huidobro's *Arctic Poems,*

cold as the decision-making
of the nation's fearless leaders,
blind as Borges but with no insight whatsoever,

cold as Pinochet
but with delusional gods and democracy
on their side.

April 25, 2007

LOOKING FOR RAQUEL WELCH

When Artemio arrives home
it's dark o'clock in the shade
and the clouds sweat rain.

At baggage claim,
a girl grabs Artemio's bag by mistake,
he points out her error,

she apologizes profusely,
her smile glistens
in the terminal long after she's gone.

Artemio hails a taxi,
the Interstate is jammed at this time of day,
the Neanderthal taxi driver

is apparently still evolving,
still surviving,
still hunting and gathering.

Artemio growls when he
gets to his destination,
and the Neanderthal growls back.

As he steps out of the taxi,
Artemio looks around for Raquel Welch,
but it's a million years too late.

April 26, 2007

THE HUNT

Raquel Welch in white bikini
in the pre-Cambrian seas
oozes onto the shore.

As she walks, pebbles knock each other down,
sunlight hammers its own disk
into a grotesque flatness.

She smiles into the dizzying sky
which avoids the shrunken wind,
the wind fights back with open legs.

It has been Artemio's dream,
hell, it has been
every man's dream.

In a rush to impregnate every female,
we get trapped by the pleasure
that simmers at the hand,

galloping antelope distract us,
spears froth in our direction,
and it is no longer clear who or what we are.

April 27, 2007

DISCARDING BEAUTY

Spears bounce off the hide of the enemy,
stone axes spark and chip,
fire must be re-invented every day from water.

She pulls the sinew off with her thighs
while she's wearing a T-shirt that says,
"One Million Years, BC"

Of her race: They drank the cave
in altitude,
they spared religion, wrongfully.

They speared each other
as harbingers,
appalled in dust and boulder.

If beauty was tossed aside,
well, it landed at Artemio's feet
just today,

and it is not something
he can use,
it is not something he needs.

April 28, 2007

HOW TO HANDLE FICTION

What does a smile mean to the stones,
to the troglodytes, to the man who has everything
except Raquel Welch's womanhood?

Artemio fights off a caveman,
pulls another by the hair,
clubs another one to death.

Raquel befriends a pterodactyl,
because what charms a man
will also charm a creature.

What plans we have
reveal themselves on the wall,
a saber-tooth, a trilobite

snag in our nets of spleen.
An exclamation in Raquel
floats on the surface in ruins,

her outfit torn apart by lust.
The win can come
from other centuries.

Artemio sees his reflection
in the still sea,
salt coating the pyramids,

each wall made up of blocks
which father other blocks.
Raquel touches his reflected shoulder.

The jellyfish and angel fish, startled,
scatter from the pier
as an ancient tennis ball washes ashore.

PART TWO

CRINGING AT THE MENTION OF CANDY GÁMEZ

Making love to Candy Gámez
has become a desert,
Gila monsters roll their eyes quizzically.

Caressing her in an abandoned classroom
at the University of Nebraska, 1971,
snowflakes clinging to the windows,

peering like nuns,
the wind made noises like lovers.
Artemio drinks water from a canteen,

the red mesas rise like pennies.
Indians claim that this is their land,
but Artemio shoos them away.

The scorpion of his love for Candy
curls its tail in self defense,
the stone of his heart

radiating heat into a nearby century plant.
Oh, God, the yin and yang of a machine
yet tells time.

The clouds have fallen to the desert floor
and have become fossils
in Artemio's thighs.

April 27, 2007

DAUGHTER

A woman takes off her arms,
go ahead, look inside, she says.
Artemio peers inside,

ah, the lungs, the beating heart,
the stomach full of menudo,
and lower down, the womb.

He cranes his neck
and is able to see
out of her vagina.

He urges her
to put her arms back on.
She obliges.

It finally dawns on Artemio
that this is Candy Gámez.
Is this her revenge?

Why couldn't she be
like most women,
and just demand child support?

She pushes Artemio's daughter in his face.
His thirty-seven year old daughter
shuffles her feet like a little girl.

There is no way to make amends
short of going back in time,
and even the present is irretrievable.

April 27, 2007

BIG RED NEBRASKA SHARKS

Back in the Fifties
Artemio's old third grade teecher
Miss McMurdock always told us mexicans

"never capitalize mexican!"
Artemio was too young to understand,
went on and procreated,

remained unaware till now.
It seems one day his daughter
showed her mother a book of poems

she was reading. She was writing poetry, too,
and she told her mother
she liked the way this poet wrote.

After agonizing weeks,
Candy finally told her daughter
that the poet she admired so much

was actually her father. He's your father.
Her daughter was excited and stunned,
and that's how she ended up

on Artemio's doorstep.
The maelstrom of modicum
upon her shy face,

fracturing Artemio in half.
Grandchildren circled the old man
like shark fins.

THE COLLECTOR OF CITIES

The radio towers on the round mound
of Las Cruces collect the dust
which used to be claimed by Indian noses.

The wind sheds its skin and moves on,
a simple act of dryness
breaks apart before your very eyes.

Artemio dozes off as Cecilio
drives the pick-up truck
to Austin, Texas thirty years ago.

Artemio and Cecilio were going
to meet José Ángel Gutiérrez,
but Artemio can't remember why.

Time cramps up like the muscles
in a woman's lower extremities,
the past sneaks up on the past,

and bites its head off.
In the distance,
El Paso pretends to be white.

Artemio takes the landscape in his hand,
folds it and re-folds it
until the metal melts in his fist,

it pours out molten between his knuckles.
After it cools
it becomes the same landscape as before.

Buildings demand the flesh
noone has anymore.
Apparently, we've arrived at our destination.

April 27, 2007

MISS BRAZIL

Artemio's compadre & comrade Ernesto Cardenal
once asked, rhetorically, of course,
"And you, what do you want?

To go to bed with Miss Sweden or Miss Brazil?"
If Artemio had a choice
he would choose Miss Brazil,

if she was nice and brown,
if she came with money or land.
Or, at least, a mother worth looking at.

He'd take her for a ride
in his punch-you-in-the-face blue GTO,
stick shift, kickass motor,

never mind the bleeping polease,
dem hillbilly Texas cops always eating
BBQ donuts at Deputy Dog's Donert Shoppe.

Yes, indeed, Artemio would choose Miss Brazil's
sculptured body, marvelous breasts,
and those beautiful buns,

but, most of all, Artemio would choose Miss Brazil
because of the cute way she says
she'll work for world peace if she wins.

May 2, 2007

THE RIDDLE

Artemio was helping Noah gather pairs
for the Ark, two of everything,
venturing far and wide,

into valleys, mountains, deserts,
paradises, lavish palaces, ghettos.
You get the picture, don't you?

Anyway, Artemio brought back a gay couple,
man and man, a lesbian couple,
woman and woman.

But, Noah said no, we don't need them.
And, so, when the collection was finished,
and the rain started coming down,

everything on earth perished
except for what Noah
had crammed into the Ark.

May 7, 2007

FLEA FLICKER

In the Seguin High School stadium
a black boy outruns all the white boys
into the end zone for a touchdown.

This is right after they integrated
the schools in Seguin.
The Mexicans around Seguin

had no football savvy,
or, at least, that's what everyone
was led to believe.

Artemio had no talent
for any sports, indeed, no talent whatsoever,
though sometimes his poems appeared in *The Cricket.**

Yet, the two hundred pound defenders
were no match for him, the linebackers
stood stunned, their hands on their hips,

a dumb, puzzled look
on their stupid faces, thinking,
stinking Mexican sure has a way with words!

May 11, 2007

*Seguin High School student paper

CHICANO ICE AGE

Artemio wipes off his club,
hair stuck to his fingersnails
from having pulled the animal

across dirt and rocks.
The sky, dinosaur-blue,
echoes with the sound beasts

intent on taking their toll.
Artemio skins the saber-tooth tiger
that almost took his life,

the teeth will be his trophies.
He will not share it
with the shaman.

Artemio mixes pigments
to celebrate his victory
on the cave wall.

The others huddle at the entrance,
their furs flutter
in the chill wind.

Long, dirty matted hair
meticulous to the pellets of ice
that begin to fall.

May 4, 2007
2:00 PM-2:07 PM

MADRE

Artemio's mother lies at the cemetery
just above Geronimo Creek.
The trees stretch their arms,

but they cannot reach her with their shade.
The clouds dip down but lose their crown,
the sun tries its best to brighten her day,

but it is ninety million miles away.
Failure, failure is what one would expect.
The birds whistle their songs for her,

the mockingbird wears out its beak.
Hell, the son-of-a-bitch even learns to speak.
Alas, only the ornithologists seem impressed.

Artemio's mother lies at the cemetery
just above Geronimo Creek,
the boards of the old bridge used to rattle

to let her know Artemio was on the way
for one of his rare visits.
Unfortunately, the county has gone

and built a brand new bridge.
The dead don't like surprises,
so Artemio bangs two boards together

just as he approaches with flowers
and a Virgen de Guadalupe candle.
The new bridge looks confused.

May 15, 2007
2:46 PM-2:58 PM

THE FOG

(Artemio, five years old)

Artemio's mother helps him with his underwear
(hand-made by her from flour sack material)
as Artemio lifts one foot

and then the other
next to the wood-burning stove
to stay warm.

His Uncle Juan and Aunt Duvina
stand around and wait.
At this point the fog

of the ancient past does not lift.
Triceratops might as well prowl outside.
Martians and their ray guns

could be annihilating earthlings.
Out in the fields of corn
that grow today,

perhaps, perhaps Artemio could put
that whole day back together.
What a treasure it would be!

May 16, 2007

THE GLORY THAT WAS ROME
AND THE GRANDEUR THAT WAS GREECE

After Artemio's mother died in childbirth,
Artemio's father, the gutless wonder,
found a new love

and this new love convinced him
to move to California,
"Let's move to greener pastures…," she told him.

And they moved to Thermal, California.
Surfing desert if you ask me,
Artemio would have said,

he wasn't smart enough to know better.
So they moved to Beverly
like in that old hillbilly TV show.

But, Artemio was a little Jethro
left behind with his grandparents.
No cement pond, no palm trees, just these memories

which provided substance,
which lay the foundation.
Rome wasn't built in a day.

May 17, 2007

KINGSBURY STREET BLUES

Artemio sucked at pinball
in the pre-Chicano days
of Kingsbury Street

where one of the Nieto twins
was killed by a car,
where Artemio courted

one of their sisters.
The musk still present
in his nostrils.

These decadent years later
Artemio hears that
she has died of cancer,

died young like her mother.
Heartbreak does not heal heartbreak,
and now even Kingsbury Street has died,

except for the chicken feathers
which escape the Tyson chicken plant
and float to the local college.

Oh, God, for such an education
to finally solve the riddle.
What came first, the chicken or the egg?

VATOS LOCOS

El Louie had not been a friend to Artemio.
Actually, Artemio didn't care for the vato,
he ran with a different crowd.

El Louie and his gang
thought you had to be
a macho to be a man.

Sometimes that will
run you afoul of the law,
and of your own strict rules, Artemio warned.

So they buried El Louie
and on the third day
he rose to heaven.

God (otherwise known as Chuy)
somehow found it in his heart
to forgive Louie all his faults,

and they were many.
God found a dirty little corner
where he put troublemakers like El Louie.

And to this day the vato stands there
collecting dust and spiders
along with the other vatos locos.

May 4, 2007

BRIDGE OF SIGHS

Artemio's hometown, which has a total
of twenty-seven hundred bridges,
has decided to get rid of every single one of them.

They will be imploded,
they will show it live on TV. Bridges that span
the Colorado River, all the I-35 bridges,

bridges that traverse Walnut Creek.
And what is the purpose
of all this bridge destruction, you ask?

Well, it's not that hard to figure out.
The city council has hit upon the idea that
it can get rid of the homeless by destroying their "homes."

ARTEMIO'S ATTIRE

The katun of cool came and went,
Artemio none the worst for wear,
square and squarer still,

long hippie hair or leisure suit,
Army pants, patchwork quilt jeans,
Artemio all the same.

Always casting an eye
on the human pre-condition,
almost as if he wasn't human himself,

his pelt hung on him by evolution,
the kind of evolution
man will never understand,

but, Artemio thinks he's caught a glimpse,
in the dense jungle, in the bare desert,
in the crowded cities, in abandoned towns.

Yes, the streets of town empty,
except for the asphalt,
and a horned-toad that scampers across it,

looks at Artemio in the eye
at high noon
like a desperate Gary Cooper.

May 5, 2007

THAT'S ARTEMIO

That's Artemio leaning against
the back bumper of a 1954 Chevy
holding his toy Indy race car.

He was six in that black & white photo,
wearing only shorts, no shirt, barefoot,
he would not wear shoes

until he started first grade
at the ripe old age of ten.
Why do you think he's illiterate?

Uses too many commas,
doesn't know when to use
that and which.

That's Artemio before he realized
he would grow up to be Chicano,
before he realized he'd become a poet.

The '54 Chevy is parked in front
of his maternal grandmother's house on Hidalgo St.,
the crooked little house still stands there today,

straighter than the slouching,
hunchbacked, and deteriorating Artemio.
But, who would believe Chevy was vulnerable?

IDENTITY THEFT

If Artemio had any sense of identity,
it was buried in the deep past,

stone pyramids did not enter into it,
Mexican revolutions, dead stadiums,

guerrilleras not part of it either,
brazeros zilch, algodón cotton,

campesinos nel, chasing the crops
in canvas-covered trucks not important,

yet words of all sorts humbled him,
beckoned him, torn like a weed

from the ground, the weed clutching
the stony clods of dirt,

Artemio unknowingly accepted the air,
wore the sky like a shirt,

did not call the sun by its Aztec name,
gave it his own foul name,

gave everything a dirty name,
if Artemio had any sense of identity,

it lay within, and without—
sole surviving son of la pinche Malinche.

MEETING
MR. INCOGNITO
2010

MEETING MR. INCOGNITO

We go to hear a poet at Columbia,
you say he's the best, but when we get there,

I realize it's a goddamn Soviet poet,
he talks about oppression

as if it was something bad,
he makes Siberia seem so cold,

Mandelstam died in a prison camp, he says. Nyet!
I'm gaga over a college girl in the third row,

eyes which flash of scholar, but echo princess,
I will be your czar, baby, baby, baby...

The poet signs his book for you,
what kind of name is Mr. Incognito?

I stink therefore I am (a line from one of his poems).
Green eggs and ham (my line, of course).

I'd rather eat the lamb and Mary, too (again, my line),
but has anybody noticed I'm fixated on the princess.

Have you come in your panties yet?
I blurt out in my head at you,

else you slap me silly, while your hero
sounds more like a truck driver than a poet.

COFFEE KLATCH

We're invited to the Dark Ages,
the Black Plague, actually, it's a Starbucks,

where you and your poet friends
can continue sucking the blood out of poetry

like mosquitoes, Dracula, or leeches.
No, no, not leeches — they're the cure.

Mr. Incognito is a proud and boastful
son of a bitch, all them Russians are,

but you and the rest of his groupies
cannot see that he's a pathological dictator,

waiting for his statue to be cast.
Suddenly I notice that the girl

from the third row has showed up, too.
My coffee starts flapping wildly in the cup,

sugar runs around with its head cut off.
At this moment I could drink

whatever Socrates is drinking.
I run up and down the Acropolis,

right now, it's just an anthill.
I swing my sword at their antennae,

find your way home now, I shout,
not knowing they find their way

by other means, superior to ours.
She looks my way, I pretend I don't see her.

The Russian sees her, too.
He looks at me and reads my mind,

it's not that hard for a man
to read another man's mind

when it comes to women.
Anything else is a lost cause.

That's why we rape and pillage,
and never get along.

FOR DEBORAH

I finally work up the courage
to go talk to her,

her name is Deborah Silverfine,
not Debbie, she says.

I think it's not a matter of life and death,
after all, what's in a name?

Where have I heard that before?
We chit chat while she waits her turn

to talk to the great man.
Her short skirt reveals beautiful legs.

I fire up the acetylene,
she wakes up the welder in me,

she hands me my hardhat,
this is New York after all, ain't it?

I stare at her cleavage,
and realize I'm a lecher,

and then she gets her chance
at Mr. Incognito.

My fifteen minutes of fame are over.
Get it through your head, Andy Warhol is dead!

DREAM ON

You excuse yourself from the Second Coming,
and come over to my table,

I'm the runner-up, second is the first loser,
like they say in racing.

I ask you if you had a good time?
Your eyes are still sparkling.

You smile and say,
yes, I had a great time.

You say goodbye to your friends.
I glance over at Deborah,

she doesn't know I'm alive.
Who was your little friend?

I pretend ignorance.
We ride the subway home.

WELCOME HOME, KOTTER

You take cold plums from the refrigerator.
"Hey, grab a soda for me,"

I tell you from the couch.
I open the laptop,

check my email, google Deborah Silverfine,
she's got pictures online.

I surf away before you waltz into the living room.
You sit down and put your hand on my thigh,

hand me my soda, you look tired.
I'm halfway up a cliff

before I realize I'm not Stallone.
You look at the signed book,

signed by God himself.
I keep my mouth shut.

There is nothing between us
except the dark matter science has been searching for.

FUGUE

In the morning, New York seems so refreshing,
its skyline could conquer the world, if only.

But then, if you look close,
you start seeing the creepy crawlers,

things you'd never find in an Egyptian museum,
American teenagers destroying Stonehenge,

the homeless ply their gladiolas,
kittens set afire by cops,

Mafia grandmothers who spat out their babies
through the anus,

a blind saxophonist blocks the sidewalk,
better walk on the street,

concentrate on the skyscrapers,
they're scraping the sky clean, at least.

THE ERRAND

A limping jet heads to La Guardia,
I see the smoke from an engine,

I see it disappear behind the houses,
I know it lands safely

because the news concentrates
on the Governor and his high-priced whore,

the sun empties its feet,
a seagull paints the gates of sand,

a cop beats a black man on the curb,
the kind of cop can't spell décor.

What was it I was supposed
to buy at the grocery store?

Bread, milk, tomatoes,
Hannibal's elephants,

a piece off the plane
that struck the towers,

the titillating dragons of yore,
and a box of Kotex.

I drive home with the power windows down,
the wind sits in the passenger seat.

REYES BUELLER'S DAY OFF

I was supposed to work on my paper
about pre-industrial cities,

instead I meet you for lunch
a subway and a taxi ride away,

the heretics in business suits,
the incandescent office girls

contrast with non-descript human beings
who tallow and twist about,

a holocaust of hot asphalt in their teeth,
I breathe the space between them,

and then I realize I've been looking
directly at the boxing glove of your smile

in the delicatessen window, you wave,
I wave back, it's a great day off.

THE LUNCH

You tell me how I always have
that lost look on my face

of a villager in Metropolis
in search of someone to save him,

super heroes having to keep the thugs away.
I order my sandwich,

a Philly cheesesteak,
we talk the meaningless things

we talk about at every lunch.
Outside, the city deepens,

I ask for cushions so we can
sit up higher,

the city lowers, I ask for more cushions.
Then you tell me you gotta go,

I kiss you goodbye.
In the subway I become a dolphin,

thumping away the sharks
from my standing position,

or at least I imagine so,
still trying to be your hero.

STARLET

When I get home, I turn on the news.
The Chinese government blames

the latest riots on a group
of criminal elements,

and not even the government
believes its own lies.

I certainly won't watch the Olympic games,
that would only offer support

to those little runts
(excuse my French).

Confucius would be confused,
and confounded

by his modern day fellow men,
and condone earthquakes and floods

in his blonde wig,
putting on Hollywood airs,

even going so far
as wearing Sharon Stone's panties.

DREAM SONG

In this dream I have, the Germans
are indeed a super race,

they wear the best shoes,
the best suits, they have

the best weapons, the best missiles,
the best gas ovens,

the rest of my dream
is kind of sketchy.

Why the hell would they befriend
the stupid Italians?

What dumb General
lead them into Africa?

Questions beget questions,
and soon the super race

becomes as scummy as the other races.
I woke up, got a cold drink of water,

listened to your girlish snoring,
you were exhaling blank molecules

which fell back to earth
at Tungaska.

WAR GAMES

"That girl's standing right there,
and you're talking about her back door!"

"Mr. Potato Head, Mr. Potato Head,
back doors are not secrets!" the big guy

yells at the skinny curly-haired nerd.
Do you have to watch that movie

every time it comes on,
while shaking your head in an amused,

mock disgust? Yes, I guess I do,
I tell you without turning away

from the TV, and the world does not end
in Global Thermonuclear Warfare.

Sometimes I wonder why it didn't.
Both sides were poised for it, what a pity.

In elementary school I hid
underneath a desk made of lead, I was told.

TWENTY LOVE POEMS AND A CARTOON

I see you are reading Neruda
as I climb into bed and wrest the remote

away from you. "Hey, hey," you tell me.
"But you're reading that stupid book."

I look at you in amazement.
"Besides that's a re-run, one of

billions and billions of *Law and Order*
re-runs, more than there are stars

in the night sky, the day sky,
the Martian sky, and Marvin

trying to blow up each and every one of them."
I turn over on my side, go to sleep defeated.

Bugs Bunny foils the attempt—
where was he when the towers fell?

THE UNITED NATIONS BUILDING

Remember that ferry which crashed into the pier,
and the skipper got fired,

and his first mate Gilligan seemed too sailory?
How many times have we boarded that ferry

to cross the Mersey to the cobbled hills,
the morning sun shining

like a red rubber ball
and showing off its petticoats,

the fog never escapes its own moisture,
the wind as far away as Russian wind?

I read the *New York Times*
to shed my fists,

astronauts in a capsule
must feel foolish now.

I don't want to toot my own horn,
but isn't the United Nations Building

getting way too close,
I see foreign fellows in the windows,

I point to them, this is my girl,
they acknowledge you with purple hands.

THE FAILED POET

She's not in the room right now,
let's talk, she refers to herself

as a failed poet, she's writing a novel now,
every character is beautiful

until the second chapter, second paragraph.
The clouds taste sweet,

the sun is not wearing its hat,
the heroine has to steal smiles,

her ears are silver, the stolen smiles
have no idea that poetry

has been postponed, come to a stop,
vamoose, goodbye, so wrong,

a Beatles song does not inspire,
I figure she will overcome.

THE SLUSH

The city is caught in the grip of ice,
and New York City snow,

snow unlike any other,
you, yeah, you, Eskimo, you got a name for it?

The sleighs fleece tourists
in Central Park regalia,

the crows pull their coats on tighter,
pigeons pretend they are warm,

I hold your gloved hand
as we hurry into the pizza joint,

the cold beer counteracts the cold.
The ice crunches underneath my shoe

until it finally melts like the Poles.
Big chunks of Antarctica

maneuver up the Hudson,
obviously lost, right-wingers forbid the warming.

We bundle up as we go outside,
snowflakes cling to your eyelashes,

you blink and they fall off —
the wonder of it all.

BACH

A homeless beggar pulls Bach
unknowingly from dirty snow,

you give him the dollar I begrudge you,
but get over it like I always do

when you go out of your way.
The buildings of New York, proud peacocks

in the wrong season, of course,
(but what season isn't wrong?)

your eyes sparkle new stars,
your smile has left the door open,

I feel ashamed of being
so selfish all the time like most men.

We take a taxi
to the bridge, off in the distance,

the Statue shines its light of branches
and roots into the mud

that makes its way
underneath your majestic little feet,

to where it runs into bedrock,
and the Flintstones hoot and holler.

LEATHER JACKET

I love the way you bend your knees
to wipe after you pee,

there's something so sexy about it,
you catch me looking at you,

the me with far-off eyes, you smile,
perhaps not every man is incorruptible,

but I am, I am when it comes to you.
You tell me we're going to a movie,

a chick flick I assume,
but you know I never complain,

the old, over the hill stars
Jane Fonda, Goldie Hawn, Diane Keaton,

always have young starlets
play their daughter,

and of course I treasure the view
of Cameron Díaz in panties,

or Drew Barrymore topless.
Are you ready yet, you startle me.

I tuck in my shirt,
grab my leather jacket —

don't know what animal died
to keep me warm and stylish.

THE GHOSTS

I look up and think I see the Towers,
you look like you've seen a ghost, you tell me,

yes, the ghost of three thousand people
I want to tell you, but I can't,

I don't want to trouble you
with life and death,

after the nice evening we've had,
dinner, a movie,

the up to now beautiful New York night
possible only in New York.

The subway ride home is quite pleasant,
two thugs seemed occupied

with the booty from petty theft no doubt.
A man in his sixties

hands in his overcoat,
his eyes fixed on the floor.

Can he see all the way to China,
the cruelty of the Chinese government?

Suddenly the thugs stand up for their stop,
come on grandpa,

they coax the sixty-year-old man,
I smile at myself

for always thinking the worst
as I look at our passing reflections in the windows.

STEREO

After the subway, we walk in the parking lot
to our car, the driver's side window is broken,

the radio is gone, the cds,
even your favorite umbrella

which you should have taken with us.
What kind of pansy thieves

would take an umbrella? you cry,
and lean your head on my shoulder.

The cops arrive after an hour,
take the report,

the male and female public servants
even now would like to be handcuffed

to donut shops far and wide,
and not be standing here in the cold night,

seeing their own breaths and ours,
the stars hanging like metal in the sky.

We drive home in silence,
the streets hold back the frozen trees.

MR. INCOGNITO'S AMERICANIZED GOBBLEDYGOOK

AS I LAY DYING

Why does Dylan Thomas look at me
as I go gentle into that good night?

Why does Robert Lowell run out of juice
every manic Monday?

Why did Sylvia leave a note on the refrigerator,
"Too cold to die in here"?

Why did Allen Ginsberg come to Texas
and waste his New York minute?

Drunk as hell, Ann Sexton
pinched her clitoris in anger.

RIMBAUD'S LAST LOVER

I kiss Rimbaud's festered leg,
it is the worst kind of incest,

because, you see, all poets are related.
I caress his cancer with the inside of my thighs,

I allow Verlaine to lie down and watch.
Rimbaud's sister is my sister, too,

and she pleads there in melancholy.
My mouth is tasting of Abysinnia now,

my black slaves haul goods
along the cliffs.

Still, in my feverish mind,
I do not know if I am me, or my lover.

A REMEMBRANCE OF CAL

Have you ever been with Cal
when he goes totally bonkers?

Cal once showed me Elizabeth's panties
which he pulled out of the hamper.

This fathered me a daughter,
he howls at me out of his mind.

Inexplicably, I'm turned on by his wife's
undergarment,

while Cal rails about his daughter,
how bright she is, how unlike her mother.

There's only so much you can decipher
about a thirteen-year-old girl, I tell myself,

but Cal cannot be dissuaded
when he's walked on water.

LA VIDA LOCA

When she told me she had cheated on me,
I imagined Cher spread-eagled,

and Sonny dead on the slopes.
Thank you, tree, oh thank you, tree.

Could I forsake the look of love in her eyes
while she humped another man?

It ain't me, babe, it ain't me.
The song kept grinding like an organ grinder's monkey,

and did not resolve itself.
It ain't me, babe, echoed once again.

It was Sonny's misfortune,
but you are just a whore, I hollered.

THE BELLE OF AMHERST

Do you suppose Emily would do it
the same way if she was a man?

She didn't handle trains that well,
she gave them way too many human traits.

A horse becomes Mr. Ed in her hands,
hoofs of the sacred.

She fantasized the sun because
she would not go outside.

The padre's pants
neatly folded in a letter.

She mingled limbs in boring dresses.
Her period never left a stain.

WESTERN STAR

You know the look Henry Fonda gives you
when the kid is shooting holes in his hat?

Well, that's the look your hero would give you
if that was you holding the gun.

But, you are just a poet,
and would never get that stare.

He looks down on you,
you are just a coward in his book.

He stands there and faces the Wild Bunch,
which you could never do.

He turns his back on you,
but still your knees are shaking.

Henry knows you're a big sissy,
why try to deny it, Jane?

HERBIE THE LOVE BUG

I'm driving Herbie the Love Bug,
I have a nice ass and big tits,

I'm Lindsay Lohan in a man's body.
I killed my share of Jews during the war,

I raped Italian girls on the march to Rome.
Vesuvius ain't got a thing on me.

I'm driving the streets of LA,
I'm driving Baretta to kill his wife,

I'm driving OJ to slice up Nicole and Ron.
I'm driving Sal Mineo's killer.

No one would suspect a Volkswagen of this.
I'm looking for love, that's all.

THE MASTER OF FINE ARTS

I was having a conversation with Berryman
as we were both speeding to our deaths.

I could tell his heart was not in it.
It sort of ticked me off,

wouldn't it tick you off?
I imagined Mr. Bones with a compound fracture.

Henry threw up on the way down.
I stressed the importance of my questions,

the self-importance of the self.
Suddenly, there was none.

So, kids, what have we learned?
That's why I hate teaching poetry.

THE NEW EMPEROR OF ICE CREAM

When your daughter-in-law walks into the room,
everyone smells sex and candy.

The neighbor's wife goes swimming in my pants
while her husband serves the Shiites.

I never get tired of eating cherry pie,
it's just American pie I hate.

The lecherous Dr. Smith has stowed away.
Danger, Penny Robinson.

I don't know what sank the Titanic,
but I know it was cold and sweet.

FOR MY DAUGHTER FRIEDA

Sylvia's white thighs marred by menstrual blood,
I wipe them clean, unlike the gutless Ted.

I would not let my son grow up
where boobies ride on bicycles two by two.

I yell for them to run. Run.
London Bridge is falling down,

and not even Old Possum can stop it.
I have a premonition of Middle Eastern men.

I push Sylvia's knees together
until they're on opposite sides.

ALICE'S RESTAURANT

I see Berryman checking out
a girl's ass in the restaurant.

I see Bukowski grab himself
and motion to a waitress, see.

Sylvia Plath sucks up spaghetti
while Ted sits at another table with his mistress.

e. e. cummings re-writes the menu
and orders a S A nd WI   ch.

Roethke demands his salad
be fresh and free of bugs.

Lorca walks in with a bullfighter,
and orders the Spanish dish of death.

TREES

I had the trees cut down,
the ones so much admired by Kilmer.

Today I bulldozed those two roads
which diverged in a yellow wood.

I had the Statue of Liberty
shipped off to Guantánamo.

I told Dylan's father,
go on, get the hell out of here, die already.

I set up some giant fans
to blow away the fog and the little cat feet.

I turned off the power to Whitman's house,
see if he can sing the body electric now!

THE SWEATY GARY COOPER COUPLETS

I've heard the rumors that e. e. cummings
is on the way back.

You've probably heard those rumors, too.
I'm not worried about myself,

but I'm concerned about you.
You've been stealing his stuff for years.

I know you once ran off
with Olaf glad and big.

I know you stole the bells
from his pretty how town.

I know you carried his heart
in your heart, and gave it to your girl.

You had the gall to tell her
it was your very own.

Oh, he's on the way back, alright,
and soon it's going to be high noon.

Poems From

chicanopoet.blogspot.com

2004-2010

PEDRO CÁRDENAS

For my grandfather

The past speaks for itself.
I stand outside the situation
like if I don't belong here.

The words fly of their own accord,
making themselves visible.
They appear right here.

The gulf is blue and white and brown,
eschewing the primary colors,
sort of.

The sand suspends molecular
in the salt spray and sea breeze.
Palm trees bend the downtown district.

Tall buildings jut out
from the high ground,
not much defense there.

Especially when another Carla hits.
Hopefully the statue of Selena
will be left standing.

In the aftermath of the hurricane,
my grandfather collected clothes
and canned food,

we loaded everything into a trailer
and drove it to the auditorium.
The damage in town was tremendous.

My brothers and I walked
across the street to the beach,
Valentín, Julián and Reyes.

The destruction amazed us,
and us thinking of it as a one-time thing,
still unaware of the natural world.

Coming down we were stopped
at National Guard road blocks,
my grandfather would get out and talk,

and soon we would be on our way.
Heading towards Corpus Christi,
into the eye of the storm.

The words speak for themselves,
the windowless skyscrapers looked
like a scene from *Planet of the Apes*.

A little anachronism doesn't make
too much of a difference in time —
I wish I could remember every feeling,

every thought, every emotion
that went through our young minds.
We tossed sticks and shells into the bay.

The bay was still churning
and all the breakwaters lay
like Greek ruins in the waves.

Soon we headed back inland —
losing the taste of the salt air
by the time we drove through Taft.

Back in Seguin we had stories to tell,
and oddly enough,
I didn't tell mine until today.

FOR MY GRANDSON IN THIS TIME OF WAR

I push my grandson in his Hot Wheels Jeep,
he is one and has just started walking.
He's a happy little boy.

Somewhere in the blowing sands of the Iraqi desert,
a young man loved by his grandfather
is lying dead in a sandbox a million miles from home.

Somewhere in the city of Baghdad
little children are blown apart by 500lbs. bombs.
The grandparents cannot put the pieces together.

My grandson plays in his Hot Wheels Jeep
and I pray to my wayward God.
"Never, God, never send this little boy to war!"

REBECCA OF THE RIVERS

For Rebecca and Juan

We were smoking and drinking beer,
the river flowing quietly, and at that moment
we didn't realize time was flowing too.

Time with its little brown hands
that pulls you along unawares,
dragging your hair white,

slowly taking away your ability
to write Chicano poetry and limbo
at the same time that you sucker-punch someone.

Your eyes were diamonds that
cut the summer clouds into recognizable figures.
Brown Buffaloes, caracoles...

It is only now that you are lost,
that we struggle to turn back the hands of time,
but its octopus arms escape us.

Oh, Rebecca, goddess of the rivers,
we have come bearing gifts and libations
that you appear to us

once again in your splendor
and bless Seguin with your presence,
the riverbanks are bare without you!

LOCH NESS

The wind blows across the loch,
a murky sky blows bubbles like clouds
in the direction of the shore.

I see the creature in a photograph,
like a serpent sliding on the water
on its way to a Dylan Thomas church.

I didn't use old Bobby Burns
in that last line,
not even for old times sake, ha, ha.

I hear La Llorona cry for her lost little criaturas.
Sandra Cisneros is trying to console her—
but this ain't no Woman Hollering Creek

on the highway to Seguin, Texas.
I know the creek well,
I have followed it back to its source.

It starts on a hillside
near Randolph Air Force Base—
you could say it belongs to the military!

Maybe the Air Force took La Llorona's kids,
and is using them for scientific experiments—
making white kids out of Mexicans!

WHEN I'M FIFTY-FOUR

Will I write poetry, will I write prose,
will I still dress like a salty old Sgt. Pepper
when I'm fifty-four?

Will the audience still recognize my face
in the Brown Submarine beneath the waves
of the Chicano sea?

I'm dancing a slow dance with Lucy
when skinny old-maid Eleanor Rigby
says, "didn't you used to be a poet?"

Nel, I used to be a Chicano poet,
but that was back in the days of the past,
not now that I'm fifty-four.

I once hung out with alurista, Ricardo Sánchez,
Tomás Rivera, Carmen Tafolla and Cecilio,
back when poetry cried like La Llorona.

When poetry floated like clouds
thru the Aztec pyramids built by Floricanto
in the middle of the barrio...

People ask me when I'm going to
cut my hair and grow up
and I tell them when I'm fifty-four,

and I tell them, when I become
more famous than the Beatles...
oh, I b-e-l-i-e-v-e i-n y-e-s-t-e-r-day.

THE BEST MENTES OF MY GENTE

The best mentes of my gente
have taught me that the best way to say
what's on my mind

is to use the right words,
the right sounds at the end
of each stanza.

Las mejores palabras
siempre son the most simple words.
Words that balance on their own.

The best minds of my generation
have not gone down the wrong road.
On the contrary, they have guided me

on this road that I am on.
Bad gringos bouncing off my fenders,
vendidos también.

Las mejores mentes de mi gente
always find a way
como el chino Lao.

Like my teacher Tomás Rivera
once said of the words that roam our heads.
"Don't ever try to write them down!"

I see it plainly now,
the words are within reach
and I see their innards.

I see the transparent eyes
of each bewitching word
as I grasp them and put them here.

IN MEMORY OF PETE SOLDADO

Pete died in Viet Nam
fighting for the right of the Vietnamese
to immigrate to the USA.

He spent nine days
trapped in a trench
until reinforcements arrived.

He listened
to rock and roll
and smoked dope.

He didn't
kill any babies,
he just killed the enemy,

and the enemy
killed his buddies.
He wrote down their names

in letters home
that spoke of
the horrors of war.

Pete died in Viet Nam
while unloading ammunition
at an ammo dump.

We buried Pete
in a cemetery
three blocks from his home.

His Chicano name
is carved into the granite stone
on the northeast corner of the Courthouse.

Pete died in Viet Nam
fighing for the right of the Vietnamese
to immigrate to the USA.

AMONG CHICANO SCHOOL CHILDREN

I was born on a farm.
We had no electricity,
only kerosene lamps for light,

a woodburning stove
to keep warm in winter
and to cook the pot of beans year-round.

My first day of school
I had to go barefoot,
amazed that other kids wore shoes.

They laughed at me
and I myself thought
how odd they looked with covered feet.

Mr. Patlán (a Mexican-American teacher)
took me to some store and the school district
bought me a pair of sneakers.

But, ever since that
first day of school,
I go proudly barefoot in my Chicano soul!

PAPALOTE STATE OF MIND

Sometimes you cannot believe
everything you hear.
You ask for proof

and there is no pudding.
They serve you
beans and tortillas

because that's
what we eat
down here.

I think therefore I am
said the Great Chicano Thinker
alurista

as he unwrapped
the mummy of Aztlan
on the kitchen table.

We ate of it
like a frozen woolly mammoth
eaten by Russian scientists.

We ate of it
but Aztlan remained
a castle in the clouds.

Therefore this poem pours out
like lava from the famous
volcano of Papalote.

Lava, lava
burning bright on the coastal plain
where the pyramids rise

to sacrifice the clouds.
They tear the heart
out of the sky

and it becomes
the Aztec sun
to the believers.

But I drink my Hippo soda water
and pen this poem
on the forehead of Lady Bird Johnson.

I sell used computers
at the Papalote Mall,
they're loaded with Win98 in Spanish.

Some weekends
they sell like hotcakes,
sometimes they sit on the shelves like my books,

the wisdom spilling out
of them
like Frank Lloyd Wright houses.

These period pieces
of the Chicano Movement
block Highway 181

and you can't get
to Sinton or Taft.
Who's going to pick the cotton?

My poems
engulf the Papalote Mall
like the Blob.

But I hide
inside my pickup truck
until the Brown Berets rescue me.

Till then I breathe
like the Gill-Man
and listen to the oldies.

It's Freddy Fender
or Little Joe y la Familia
trumpeting the arrival

of Lalo
and the 25 pieces
of his Chicano mind.

Stupid America,
let this poem that's stuck in your throat
bring you freedom once again!

TO MY GRANDSON

Sometimes a son can't reach the lofty goals
a father sets for him,
sometimes the grandson is called upon
to carry on the dreams.

I tried to be a great writer, grandson,
not for fame or glory,
not to enlighten the world — but me.
And I am still trying!

Along the way you try to do some good,
it doesn't have to be that much,
but it's got to be at least a little.
Every little bit helps, you know.

Just try your best to write
the greatest poem you can make out of your life.
It doesn't have to rhyme
and it doesn't have to reason.

As you can see already,
anything you write will be better
than anything your grandpa has written.
So pick up that crayon, boy!

THE ELEMENTS OF JUAN SEGUÍN

He fought
for the independence
of his land,

he was
a citizen
and a warrior,

but when
the war
was over

they buried
him
across the river.

A century later
they
bring him back home.

They bury
him there
on the side

of Police Hill,
named so
because

the police station
used to
be right there

where
I
point.

He's buried
underneath
the oak tree

that was
already
a hundred years old

when
the white
man

first infested
this part
of Texas.

JUAN SEGUÍN ELEMENTARY

I was
not born
in Papalote,

long ago
I was born
and raised

in Seguin,
Texas,
Aztlan.

My barrio
had gravel
streets,

only the
white side
of town was paved.

At the
Palace Theater,
if you were

black or brown
you had to
watch movies

from the balcony.
Whites went
to white schools.

Blacks went
to black schools,
and Mexicans

went to
Mexican schools.
I went

to Juan Seguín
Elementary,
there by the creek.

The only
white kids
I knew

when I was
growing up
were Dick and Jane.

WHEREIN I CHALLENGE THE ROYAL CHICANO AIR FORCE TO A DOGFIGHT

We had an
abandoned chicken coop
in the backyard

and on the roof
I fashioned
a helicopter cockpit.

The military
training flights
took them over our house

and back
to their base
in San Antonio.

Every afternoon
I'd climb onto the chicken coop
and don my pilot's suit

and talk into
an old army surplus
microphone.

I trained
and trained and trained
to earn

my pilot's wings
that I use now
to pilot this very poem

into my childhood
and back
with such precision.

GROWING UP CHICANO WITH
EMILY DICKINSON TALENT

Because I would not bow down for them
they kindly beat me up
and sent me off to jail,

the paddy wagon
held but just myself
and every Chicano in Aztlan.

We passed the schools
where whites could learn,
we passed the fields where only Chicanos worked.

We passed the Aztec sun
and tried to make our way up
as they kindly beat us down,

but somehow we surmised
the white man was a horse's rear
towards immorality,

and we continue
to fight the good fight
that you shouldn't have to fight in America.

GET OFF OF MY CHICANO CLOUD

The Death Star
shoots its laser
and Alderaan is gone.

Chunks of Aztlan
float in space.
Gringo asteroids

head towards
the spinning sun.
Chicanos take refuge

on Tatooine.
They're used to
scraping a living

to get by.
The Crazy Gypsy,
Omar Salinas,

rambles on
about golden robots.
There's a smell of tiny robots

that look
like trash cans.
Get a grip, Omar, get a grip.

But, Omar's moonwalking
backwards
on the desert,

little clouds
of dust rise
from his shoes

and in those clouds
a thousand ancient
civilizations thrive.

DRIVING TO AZTLAN

When AMC came out
with their Pacer
(that little

Jettson-looking car)
Carmen rushed
out to get one.

It was purple
like the
purple people-eaters.

On one trip to Austin
the radio put out waves
of Juanita Mitchell,

the hissing
of the summer barrios
became louder and louder

like La Llorona llorando,
crying over spilt
breast milk.

We saw her children
rushing the interstate,
their heads

shaped like
the pyramid of the sun,
their obsidian hair

became dull and less
menacing only after
the song ended.

We pulled into Austin
just before
Chicano poetry arrived.

**HERE I AM IN MY BIRTHDAY SUIT AT FIFTY-SEVEN,
IT AIN'T A PRETTY SIGHT (READ: SITE)**

Today is my birthday,
I turn fifty-seven,
still hanging

in there.
Lost some good friends.
When I write

this or that
I think
"Hey, Cecilio would

appreciate these Chicano colors."
Or I say to myself,
"Hey, Jim

would like the
shaman feelings
in this poem."

Or I say,
"The Chicano Kid, Max,
must be writing up a storm."

So, I keep on
writing my Chicano poems
though

maybe no one
is listening,
maybe Chicano poetry

does not reach
young Chicanos
anymore,

and if it reaches them
maybe they
don't care.

But, after
fifty-seven years
what else can I do?

So, here it is,
another Chicano poem,
brown like me,

willing to
stand alone
if need be,

because standing
alone is part
of being Chicano,

or at least
it used
to be.

Today is my birthday,
I turn fifty-seven—
horseshit, pass by!

MY AZTEC PRINCESS

Soon it will
be your birthday
once again,

my brown
Aztec princess.
I was so foolish

way back then
to think
that you would be mine.

Of course
I was just
one of the workmen

who carried stone
to the base
of the pyramid.

This pyramid
that will
honor you

for centuries
to come
with it's glory,

the sun
melting on
each stone.

Each stone
turning to
the gold

that the stupid
Spaniards
could not find.

CHAMACO'S HOMEMADE GIRL

The sixteen-year-old
Palestinian girl,
bombs strapped

under her breasts
to hide the bulge,
walks into the pizza place

and triggers the bomb.
There's no sound,
no pain.

That was easy,
everything became nothing…
They find pieces of her,

her hair, skin, brain matter
mixed with pizza,
stuck on a chair,

but they find that
her mind
is still intact

and lying on the floor.
Her thoughts
are there

for all to see,
but all of us, every single one of us
looks away

before we
start thinking
what she's thinking.

DREAMING IN COLORS

She's dreaming in colors,
she's dreaming
in brown.

My princess is brown,
Mexican, Tejana and proud.
For a thousand years

she has endured the oppression
by the Spaniards,
by the white man,

by men of her own color.
My princess is brown,
and she's lived with oppression

and discrimination and rape
all of her brown life.
She's always dreamed

of a better life.
So, every night she dreams in color,
she's dreaming the color brown.

She's dreaming the dream coming true,
she's dreaming as hard as she can.
She's dreaming in colors — all of them brown.

CALCETINES

We were so poor
when we were growing up,
Christmas meant

a pair of socks for me,
and that was it.
My uncle Frank

and Aunt Luisa
gave me those socks
once a year

whether
I needed them
or not.

These were not the socks
from Neruda's
"Ode To A Sock,"

these were not
Kafka's
insect socks,

these were not
sock drawers
in a Borges mirror,

these were plain and simple
brown, Chicano
socks.

Now all
I needed
was zapatos.

I AM JOAQUÍN, TAMBIÉN

I am Joaquín,
not Steve McQueen,
not Juan Seguín,

sometimes you gotta
tell it like it is,
not give a piss,

sometimes you make enemies
when you tell the truth,
ask Doctor Ruth.

I am Joaquín
and though Corky's gone,
always address him as Don.

Don't call me Mister,
don't call me Señor, don't tell me
La Malinche was a whore.

I am Joaquín,
not Don McLean,
American Pie don't mean beans,

the red white and blue
applies only to one color
and only if you got the dollars.

I am Joaquín,
say what you will,
do what you want,

it won't change a thing,
don't put up a fight,
I won't lose sight!

I am Joaquín,
I have a one track mind,
I won't put up with your kind!

CICATRIZ CHICANA

This is the scar
right here
on her belly

where they cut
her ovaries out,
no more brown children

to run around
the apartment building,
grow up to join

the barrio gangs,
get shot,
get knifed, get beat up,

not just by punks
but by society
in general.

Every once
in a while—
an exception,

this barrio boy
or girl
grows up to write,

to battle words
just like you she says
as she pulls the jeans over her scar.

THE CICADA GIRL

For RF

The cicada girl comes around
once every twenty years,
in the hot sun,

in a white see-through dress,
in the country,
in the cities,

sensuous long hair
blowing in the wind
like magic sprinkles

transforming me
into a hungry lover,
blood pumping like the sun,

the sun misshapen
in the heat of the moment.
The cicada girl comes around

once every twenty years.
Her wings rub together like thighs
in my mind.

Twenty years is so meaningless
now that my cicada girl
is back again.

EL PACHUCO CALLED LA PLANCHA

For Dulcinea del Toboso

They used to call him
La Plancha (The Iron)
because he was

always hot
after women.
They said

you could see
the scorch marks
on their inner thighs.

These are stories
I heard in the barrio
as a kid,

don't know what
happened to
La Plancha.

Was he
Rudolph Valentino,
Casanova,

or just Sancho.
No women come forward
and say,

"Yes, La Plancha
was a hot lover!"
Another pachuco down the drain.

MR. HENRY'S NEIGHBORHOOD

Drive through my barrio now
and all you see is the new arrivals,
you can't leave your door unlocked anymore,

the Medranos, the Nietos, the Barreras,
the Acevedos, where have they all gone?
The neighborhood store is no more,

the park is a place for punks now.
Sure, I'm an old man
and you might not like what I say,

but I didn't give a damn when I was young
what makes you think I give a damn now,
you little bastards.

They glare at me as I drive through their turf,
unaware that nothing is theirs,
that the landlord tags their behinds while they swagger.

Drive through my barrio now
and all you see is the new arrivals,
their roots are flying in the wind.

HOW YOU CREATED A CHICANO POET

Growing up Chicano
watching *Captain Kangaroo*,
going to the drive-in movies to see Lash LaRue,

going to the all Mexican school,
speaking Spanish in the schoolyard,
forced to speak English in the school room,

going back to the farm on the school bus,
white kids picking on me,
kicking me as I walked down the aisle—

I'd kick those little bastards back
and bite them if they weren't quick enough.
I haven't changed much in the intervening years!

HENRY RACCOON

Somewhere in the Black Hills of Papalote
there lived a young Chicano
named Henry Raccoon.

One day his ruca ran off
with some desgraciado,
this ain't kosher, this ain't cool, he cried.

Henry said I'm gonna get that vato
so he traveled to that brown town,
he checked into a room

above the cantina
only to find Janay Gideon's Bible
surrounded by the sinning God.

Henry had his pistolas and was prepared
to shoot off the pendejo's bolas
even if the puto had none.

He found the treacherous lovers
dancing a polka in the cantina.
The conjunto played accordions accordingly.

But, the rival was quicker than Henry to the draw
and we saw
what a bullet can do to you!

They carried Henry upstairs to his room,
everyone said it would be his tomb
but Henry recovered way too soon

which just goes to prove—
you can't keep a Chicano down on the farm
even if he comes to harm.

I THOUGHT I HEARD ABELARDO

I thought I heard Abelardo
shout twenty-five pieces
of his Chicano mind.

I thought I heard raulsalinas
rattle the bars and climb the walls
to freedom.

I thought I saw Ricardo Sánchez
on the streets of Amsterdam
wearing wooden cowboy boots.

I thought I saw alurista
singing the songs of Floricanto
screaming don't step on the Pisan Cantos.

I thought I saw the Crazy Gypsy
wearing the wings of the Aztec Angel
flying in the skies of Aztlan.

Y NO SE LOS TRAGÓ LA POESÍA (LA VACOTA HENRY)

Rivera and Hinojosa
were still respected,
their Kafka insects Mexican to the bone.

Their Mallarme faun heads
cowering under porches,
under the noses of the white man.

The Rio Bravo water
dirty like the thoughts of man,
the ruins owed in Spanish.

In those days,
Henry drugged
and quite addicted to a day-dreamed Rosa

didn't give a damn,
not even after impregnating
the tabla rosa.

So, the great Chicano prose writers
showed no surprise
and the masses never were that lyrical.

But, Henry, tough as an old vaquero
never even once
thought of giving up.

FLOR Y CANTO

The allure of alurista
seemed to be enough
when he dreamed-up the Aztec sun.

It was, indeed,
a Herculean literary effort,
from the ground up.

At that time,
Henry separated poetry from poetry,
the words dressed in Godiva.

But, alurista kept the words
and their meanings
in the ancient pyramids.

The sacrifices were inevitable,
the feast on the table,
beating heart in mid-air.

The years have passed.
Now we're either stuck
with Hispanic or Latino writers.

They, of course, can never be Chicano,
that's why they fester
out in the open.

HENRY WHO

For lorna dee cee

Weldon Kees was brown as hell,
Hart Crane as well
and El Louie was afraid of la jefita,

I repeata, I repeata,
life is not what it appears to be,
at least, not to you and me.

The Aztec poet was a fallacy
invented to keep the Gary Sotos away,
but them suckers got their way anyway.

Henry cowered over his pot of beans
folding tortillas to use as spoons
in a Rio Bravo anthology.

The Papalote tecolote
muttered Who Who Who in Spanish
and wetback Poe answered, "Nevermore!"

Carmen Tafolla's freckles
belonged in junior high back then
on her skinny thighs.

La Bird hung out
with her home-girls
in a third grade Third World.

Henry himself was just a mocoso
wiping his snot with his sleeve
in Miss Turner's sixth grade class.

Later his poetry was white as hell,
Mr. Bones' as well,
but the Chicano Renaissance was around the corner

and even though he barely
grabbed onto the caboose,
Henry's never turned it loose.

THEY SENT A TAXI FOR TOMÁS RIVERA

They sent a taxi for Tomás Rivera
but he was lost in East L.A.
parece que se lo tragó la tierra.

They sent a taxi for Ricardo
but he was nowhere to be found
la muerte es un bastardo.

They sent a taxi for Max Martínez
but he was sound asleep
y se lo llevaron sin sus calcetines.

They sent a taxi for my friend Cecilio
he was in the mountains of New Mexico
pero hallaron su domicilio.

They sent a taxi for my friend Jim
but he was far away hunting buffalo
and I'll be damned if death didn't find him.

So my advice to you and to myself
is to stay put
until a taxi comes for death itself!

SELF-PORTRAIT IN A CONVICT'S MIRROR

You young punks will not remember
when the pinto poets emerged
upon the scene machine,

a toda maquina,
the knives, the bullets of the words
they were shooting from the hip.

Ricardo Sánchez, raulsalinas,
whatever their crimes
they turned into rhymes,

Hechizospells from hell,
the iron bars that held raul
and his raza in the mind jail.

When the pinto poets looked in the mirror,
they didn't see themselves —
they saw all of us!

THE CHICANO GULLIVER

I am the Chicano Gulliver
and an army of white men
tie me down to the ground,

I must do their dirty work for them,
I must slide my throat
along the shiny glass of their wives,

I must clean the toilets
of their untouchable empire,
I must build their new roads,

their new buildings, their new bridges.
I must fight their wars,
they want me to steal black silk for them.

The ropes tear into my wrists,
my ankles, my heart, my stomach.
The ropes tear into my lips.

I am the Chicano Gulliver
and an army of white men
strap me down to my own land.

EL MACHO

Sure, he killed the vato,
spent 22 years in prison,
paid his debt to society in his mind,

funny how that
didn't bring the dead guy back,
the wife the guy never had,

the children, the grandchildren,
oh, the very talented granddaughter
who never materialized

because someone pulled the trigger.
What the hell was the fight about,
proving one's manhood?

Protecting one's territory?
At least, until the rich, white land developer
turned your barrio into a baseball stadium.

LA MEJICANA

I've got donkey brains according to her.
She claimed to have corralled
Mexican Independence won.

I told her, "You're joking, right?"
But, she was serious.
"Babe, you people

will never build great pyramids again."
The anger in her face spewed Popo.
She said, "You ain't getting none,"

and I thought to myself
run, run for your single life.
I wasn't the sharpest knife.

"Ah, hell," I told my mejicana,
"I'll go with you to the diez y seis celebration."
She called me Carranza

but I was ok with it.
I was ok with anything
in her fiery, fighting eyes.

WHEN HENRY WAS GROWING UP

When Henry was growing up
he couldn't understand
the white kids,

he just assumed
that they hadn't learned
to speak yet.

But, after awhile,
he figured
they were having trouble

learning Spanish,
maybe they
just weren't too bright.

Yet, Henry didn't
make fun of them.
But, those white kids never did learn Spanish!

LIVING IN A TACO BELL HELL

Henry stole the vernacular of the Negro
because he could not foresee that Spanish
would be the sought-after language

even as far north as Minnesota,
while Mr. Bones of barbecue
remains addicted to Taco Bell

(the white man's Mexican food)
which don't taste like it should.
The authentic enchiladers belong to raulsalinas,

ain't no mincing words in the mincemeat —
it don't mean a thing
if it ain't got dem beans.

CHICANO CAPTAIN'S LOG

The Chicano Captain Kirk
is mixing chili powder, corn flour
and cilantro to kill the Gorn,

the bamboo canon flashes,
the Gorn goes down as if
it had been slapped by a giant alurista,

as if he'd been knocked off balance
by Alma Villanueva's wide naked hips
and plump derrière,

as if Sandra Cisneros had fed him bad mango,
as if La Jefita had hit him on Octavio Paz's face
with a hot palote,

as if somehow (yes, somehow)
every Chicano poet who studied under Levine
actually wrote Chicano poetry.

In the end, Kirk helps the Gorn to his feet,
and the lousy lizard stumbles away
like the smoking mirror of our past.

FOR LILLY

The new granddaughter's home.
Years have begun to pile up
like stones from Mexican pyramids,

moved by wind and sun.
Don't let the damn Spaniards
of my gray hair hurry anymore,

don't let that stinking Stephen F. Austin
of my arthritic age
advance beyond Texas,

don't let a fat, Spanish-speaking only
Sam Houston hide like a janitor in the Alamo
of my future dust.

The new granddaughter's home
and sunstones crushed by Olmec heads
blind me with tears of joy.

MONDAY, MONDAY

My mother died on a Monday, Monday,
now once a week there's a Monday, Monday.
Sunday, and then it's Monday, Monday.

Tuesday, and it was just yesterday, yesterday.
Wednesday, and it was just two days ago
and it was just two days ago.

Thursday, and it was just three days ago.
Friday, and it was just four days ago
and it was just four days ago.

Saturday, and it's only two days till Monday, Monday.
Sunday, and then it's Monday, Monday.
My mother died on a Monday, Monday.

STARTING OVER

Lupita left La Rata and moved to Houston,
Meme married a divorcee from Nuquis,
El Caballo still works at the chicken plant.

They say El Beatle moved somewhere up north
and became a writer
but, no one knows for sure.

Speedy never made it back from Viet Nam,
La Reina del Deiz y Seis at Hidalgo Hall
died of cancer last year—

so many putos had the hots for her.
But when you visit the old hometown now
only strange Mexicans stare at you from Seguin.

It's no longer nomás Yogi Berra's déjà vu.
You've become a stranger
in your own land once again!

JAILBREAK

They say El Tapón has broken out of jail,
swimming from Alcatraz to San Francisco
with a smile across his face.

His long Indian hair dripping wet,
seals doing backstrokes next to him
and El Tapón tells them,

"We're all in the same boat, carnales,
the man is trying to keep us down,
the man is always exploiting us."

Cold and shivering, El Tapón walked proudly
through the streets of San Francisco,
walked all the way to Los Ángeles,

walked all the way to Texas.
They say there ain't a white man's jail
that can hold the heart of El Tapón.

NORTEADO

The bus drops me off in the middle of nowhere.
I wait at the crossroads.
The smell of the cornstalks turns yellow.

Suddenly a cropduster appears,
and dives at me in anger,
the pilot's white scarf waving August.

I throw myself on the road
as the plane almost lands on my back.
I run into the fields for cover.

Then I see a gasoline tanker
coming up the road.
I flag it down, and inexplicably

the cropduster slams into it.
All this is happening
as if it were a movie.

The cops arrive, the ambulance approaches.
My tie flaps in the wind.
God, grant me the strength to carry on.

MARTIN STREET AND OTHER SORROWS

> *"my rims never spin*
> *to the contrary*
> *you'll find that they're quite stationary"*
> Weird Al

Was cruisin' through what's left of the barrio
in my 2007 Honda Odyssey
wearing suit and tie from the Tall Man Shoppe

and here I am only five-foot tú
going to teach my Greek class
at Our Lady of the Lake University

but first I stop on Zarzamora
to pick up pan de dulce
empanadas de calabasa y cuernitos.

I remember Bernardino Verástique,
Víctor Guerra and countless others,
Sandy and Ángela, Max, Xilo, César Augusto,

the list of the past goes on and on
my rims never spin to the contrary
my head spins stationary.

MIRADA

I knew I was Mexican
by the way white people
looked at me.

If I walked across town
the police would stop me
and ask where I was going.

If I rode my bicycle
on the wrong sidewalk
old white ladies would cry rape.

If I went out
with a white girl
both sides of the tracks would frown.

I never had an Uncle Hank
only a Tío Fidencio
no cousin Phil only primo Pablo.

Today I know I'm Chicano
by the way the Mexicans
look at me.

PYRAMIDS OF THE SON

When the towers came tumbling down,
they crushed illegals—
Mexicans, many who were well known

to Alfonso Rincón, who delivered
sandwiches and pizza to the towers
during the 1990's, he names names,

he twirls faces in his mind,
"DNA testing," he says, "cannot
tell you a damn thing about who they were!"

He lists all their occupations,
janitor, cleaning ladies, maintenance men,
messengers, and people like him

who just delivered this and that
to the doomed towers.
"Spanish is the language of the working people

in this country," he says with a curse
as Immigration leads him away from his present job
of soldering wires at a defense contractor in Austin, Texas.

HEADSTONES

The word has lost
its Chicano name in Albuquerque
ever since Cecilio left.

The word has lost
its power and pride in San Antonio
where once the Black Hat Poet pounced.

The word has lost
its brown bravado in Colorado
where Lalo's footprints waged war in the snow.

And on the dusty streets
of Gonzales, Texas, there's evidence
that Max is trying to teach us a brand new language.

MECHANIC

My father took the motor apart,
pistons, connecting rods, cam,
tossed the oil pan aside,

oil splashing all over the place,
the floor of the garage
covered in what used to power the car.

He pulled the fenders off,
the radiator, the front tires,
back tires, trunk, taillights.

It was getting dark
so he told me to turn on
the lights.

He tore out the seats,
the radio, steering wheel,
stick shift, ashtrays.

When he was done
he took a red shop rag from his back pocket
and wiped his hands.

It was then, at the age of eight
that I realized
how to write a poem.

FLACO FUENTES

Flaco Fuentes, lowly Chicano,
ate only beans and tortillas
and survived by luck.

Flaco loved the days of old,
Aztec and Maya and Olmec, too,
though he never surmised the blood.

He sighed at what was not
and dreamed of fighting Spaniards,
slashing at them with his golden sword.

He mourned his empty life,
fought abandoned gas stations
and overgrown lots.

Dreamed that his tattered clothes
clanked like armor, shoved his sword
into leafless shrubs.

He went home and wrote such marvelous words
he thought the world
would some day need.

But the days turned into years
and no one noticed when Flaco
didn't even notice them himself.

WHO WELCOMED RAUL?

In memory of raulrsalinas

Who welcomed raul
when he finally reached
those sandy shores

after having endured
that desert of a sea,
no water to drink,

not even the occasional
rain shower or vicious storm,
after having left

the Southside of Austin
on the pilgrimage
which all of us must undertake,

but which none of us can go there
having accumulated
as much unselfish work as raul,

because most of us
only worry about ourselves,
it's always me, me, me?

It's only about others
when the benefits
are laid out beforehand.

Who welcomed raul
when he finally reached
those sandy shores?

Well, I have no doubt
that Cecilio was there,
and Lalo, and Ricardo, and Trini,

and that they talked forever
on that beautiful beach,
not in language, but in poetry.

THE OTHER MEXICAN REVOLUTION

Henry muttered his Mexican Revolution
from inside a piñata.
His woman was all for him,

her fish eyes wagging that sweet smile.
But, you must know, she secretly told herself,
a Mexican can't govern caca.

She was, of course, very clairvoyant,
even though she couldn't see the future —
looking at the past

only prepares you for the same mistakes.
Henry had all these big plans for the country
but they amounted to nothing.

"My fellow Mexicans, look upon what greatness
I have created, and be amazed!"
yelled Henry Ozymandias.

PROSPECTOR

I was digging for gold in the desert
outside of Palm Springs
when I accidently dug up César Chávez.

I told him, "Nothing's changed, brother,"
and he lay back down
with my shovel still stuck in his chest.

ELEGY FOR AN AZTEC ANGEL

"Death is for the birds,"
said Salinas to Salinas.

He spoke this of himself:
crazy as a loon,

sacrificial like Aztecas,
women's breasts he always cherished,

and don't forget the drink.
"Death is for the birds," he said,

and the birds sang in his honor,
"death is for salinas, death is for salinas"*

Salinas found it funny, shut his eyes,
and took wing into the darkening skies.

birds don't capitalize

MINOR ELEGY FOR RAUL

Had a dream about raul last night,
he was telling me,

"carnal, even in Aztlan the Fat Lady sings,"
and I'm confused and ask raul,

"You mean the Fat Lady who's supposed to sing
at the end of the opera?"

"Yes, the very one!" he tells me.
That idiot sportscaster, Dan Cook

from a San Antonio TV station
coined that phrase

and never, never have I hated San Antonio
as much as I do now.

EL LOUIE'S STATE OF AZTLAN SPEECH

Nobody stuck around to hear
the rest of El Louie's speech.

Maybe his tattered, dirty suit
made people uncomfortable,

or maybe it was the fact that clumps of his hair
kept falling off while he tried to rally La Raza,

or maybe the one moldy shoe he wore
just didn't cut it anymore,

but what else do you want from the dearly departed?
At least he's trying,

which is more than can be said
for those of you who ain't dead!

HOW TO DISMANTLE A RACE

For years he was out of touch
with his race.

He came this way,
they went that way.

He pursued the past
to come to terms with the future.

They pursued the sublime—
unaware it was just beautiful slime.

They sought comfort in shiny objects
to build their nests,

no sabían that it was knives
they laid their precious nalgas on.

He pointed the way,
but not even his own shadow followed.

EL LOUIE RETURNS FROM THE DEAD

I just dropped in to see
what condition my raza was in.

I see the poets are winning prizes
left and right.

I see the fiction writers are flowering
like Flor y Canto.

I just dropped in to see
what condición my condición was in.

I walked through my old barrio,
same old gangs new younger faces.

I see you still have to protect your turf
with knives and guns.

Sure you're proud and brown,
but nobody pays attention to a clown.

The turf you fight for
still belongs to the white man.

I just dropped in to see
what condition my raza was in.

It could be the Fifties or Sixties,
except that it's Two Thousand Eight.

DREAMING OF AZTLAN GONE BAD

We are driving in your Pacer to Austin,
the reason why escapes me.

We met in the small town of whatsoever,
I said, I'll show you my poems

if you show me yours,
but then the rains came

and swept away my fellow writers,
my friends, my medals from Nam,

my farmworker sweat, my Denver days,
my Tierra Amarilla palomilla,

my Santos Rodríguez from Dallas,
my Rubén Salazar from East L.A.

Cirol, our own gente turned upon us—
the hound of Aztlan, we supposed.

THIS SIDE OF THE WESTSIDE

I loved you for your mind back then,
though probably in the hindquarters of my head

I relished the parting of thighs—
you with your poetry of and for the barrio,

junior high school girls, El Bennie's exploits,
the old ladies, the abuelitas.

The present is so different from the past.
We've come full circle yet once more,

and I love you for your mind again,
but my reptilian brain has you cornered with its tongue

and the hot San Antonio sun bounces off my hide
as I run behind a Mexican bakery on Zarzamora St.

THE BLACK HAT POET WELCOMES CECILIO INTO CHICANO HEAVEN

At that sweet time I was still alive
says the Black Hat Poet

as he recites his best poems,
now only remembered on the Westside

and the Southside, the Mexican Sasquatch
lives again, led around by the hand.

In these present times
he would find so much to ridicule,

"so many more things need fixin', mano,
so many things have gone unsaid.

I welcome you back my friend,
but I'm unsure of how you got here," I tell him.

He sees the bewilderment in my face.
"No, carnal, it is not me who needs

to be welcomed," says the Black Hat Poet,
"it is you, bienvenido,"

and he puts his arm around me —
the abrazo we know so well.

THE HARD FOUGHT ELEGY

Moments after we left my mother's funeral,
heard by no one, not even the gravediggers

whose job it was to pour the dirt over her,
the coffin started to settle,

crushing clods of dirt beneath it,
shoving a little stone or two

deeper down, until the coffin
was happy in its place.

And over the years more muffled noises
would be heard down there,

the coffin coming apart meticulously slow,
my mother's bones separating

from each other, gently sliding off
to one side, her beautiful hair

falling from her skull, still looking
for a final resting place,

and I, her oldest son, having to write this,
having chosen the wrong profession.

LOSING CANDY GÁMEZ

> *"If tomorrow never comes,*
> *why do Mexicans depend so much upon it?"*
> Quetzalcoatl Sandoval

I'm making love to Candy Gámez,
can't be more specific

other than it happened in Lincoln, Nebraska.
The snow had her name on it,

the wind had her name on it,
so did the abandoned railroad tracks,

the waitresses at the Russian Inn envied us,
and then the springtime came

with all its glory,
the snow turned into water,

and trickled down the city drains.
I called out Candy's name

all over town, went as far as Omaha,
but she was gone, oh, she was gone,

and forty years later
my heart still pines for her—

in a Mexican sort of pain
which, as you know, has no equal.

GROWING UP MONTALVO

For José

I was not who I said I was,
how could I be?

The gravel street in front
of my abuela's house

would repeat stone after stone.
The Chinaberry tree out of place

like a chino-learnt Spanish.
My friend Pete off to Viet Nam,

to be killed for who knows
what stupid reason.

Girls I chased with a stick
they broke off in my hands.

When they became teenagers
their red lips wrecked me,

I hungered for one,
God, just one!

I screamed in poetry
what did not belong in the barrio.

Keep moving, keep moving
said the asshole at bootcamp.

Just call me the Brown Hat Poet,
since I'm neither here nor there.

COTTON PICKERS

(A memory of the fifties)

The wondrous taste of ice cold water
from the wooden barrel

in the back of the canvas-covered truck
which took the campesinos

to the cotton fields,
two blocks of ice floating,

and only us kids relaxing there
while the adults dragged

sacks of cotton up and down the rows,
filled them to the opening of the sack,

came in to weigh them,
grabbed a tin of water,

picked another and another row
until the day was devoid.

THE ENCHANTED GARDEN

My grandmother had a green thumb,
she could make rocks blossom,

and petunias sprout from pebbles.
The weeds would rush away from her,

giggling and flinging clods of dirt in haste.
Bugs would never eat her plants,

instead they headed to the neighbor's yard,
hide if a bird flew overhead,

or rattle rakes in the tool shed,
an inexplicable glint in their eyes.

My grandmother had a green thumb,
the very dirt, if asked, turned into velvet.

LA CANTINA

Grandfather rolling cigarettes
on his cigarette rolling contraption,

putting the pack of Buglers
back in his pocket,

then off to the cantina, La Gloria,
where the dancing girls

charge a quarter for each dance,
you could touch their nalgas,

and they would just smile,
drunk as they were.

Us boys would be assigned the job
of walking to the beer joint

to tell him, "Grandma wants you home!"
and the dancing girls—

(remember, these are not really girls,
they're actually women in their thirties and forties,

over the hill, on the way down,
their thighs well-versed)—

these women cry in their dusty beds,
their faces buried in a pillow

while grandfather comes home
defeated by pleasure.

THE PERSONIFICATION

In the third grade, at Juan Seguín Elementary School,
I'd walk the three blocks to Markgraf's Grocery Store,

jump a fence on the side of the store,
and devour my tacos in secret, in shame.

Is that what fosters your arrogance now?
says my wife as she tries to corral me.

She doesn't much like the fact
of my political incorrectness.

I yell like Stokely Carmichael,
I rant like Raymundo Tigre Pérez.

Ten feet shorter than Ricardo Sánchez,
I take no prisoners.

Proud as I never was
when a dirty, little Mexican third grader.

PROTRACTED ELEGY FOR PETE

Pete, your body blown apart
there in the Vietnamese jungle

while I read Américo Paredes,
you with a pistol in your hands.

Two of your fingers
quivering in the mud,

next to the smoking scalp
of Tommy, the black kid from Mississippi.

One of your lips
lying next to hot shrapnel

while I kissed a Chicana's lips
at Pioneers Park,

whose name survived in my memory
for a decade, now gone,

but, remnants of you, Pete,
float above the page to this day,

expand and grow heavy
crushing me against the earth,

leaving only the scant wiggle room
I must make use of to escape.

PUSHANDO BOTONES

"Those damn gabachos!" said Al O'Cañas
when Armstrong walked on the moon,

the same Al who had led a boycott
against the King Bee Restaurant,

yeah, the one on Kingsbury Street,
Al who drove around

in a big old car with no brakes,
the monster had fins

and a push button transmission,
the botones were on the right side

of the steering wheel,
he had to push the reverse button

to stop the car,
don't remember

why he objected
to white men walking.

THE PENCIL

I was a wild, unkempt Mexican farm boy,
rock-throwing, foul-mouthed,

forced to join civilization
(start school, in other words).

In the first grade, I stabbed Esperanza
in the palm of her hand with my pencil.

Years later, when we'd become adults,
she showed me the tiny bit of lead

still embedded in her hand.
I felt no guilt because

it had been some other me
who had done that.

Yet, now in my old age, I realize I'm
still that rock-throwing, foul-mouthed

Mexican farm boy who can't be trusted
with a pencil.

ANNIVERSARY OF UNREQUITED LOVE

Heart on his sleeve for almost
forty years,

that ain't right,
what a silly Chicano,

for that is what he is,
and has always been,

no Mexican, no Mexican-American,
no stinking Latino,

God forbid he ever
accept the word Hispanic,

screw that,
oh, yes, he's loved you that long,

wearing his heart on his sleeve
has not been easy on him,

scratched up from running
into rosebushes,

spilling hot bean caldo on it
has resulted in scar tissue,

cut by sharp, hard tortillas
when times are lean,

allergic to cilantro,
that's gringo crap

says his primo Pelón,
his cousin Pelón is always right,

it all has to do with you wearing
your heart on your sleeve, he yells,

the sleeve itself torn to shreds like a piñata
which has kept its word to the bitter end.

THE FLYING MEXICAN JESUS

I was born in a manger off Huber Road
the blood of a child welcomed by burlap

the fields had been plowed under for winter
smell of bare dirt waiting for spring

next year's rain just a cocoon
the creek clogged with stones

hoosegows of judgment day put off till mañana
winter wind narrated by an ass

they threw me off the manger's balcony
I learned to fly with a thud.

LENGUA

I had a friend pull the language knife
out of my back

only to have him confess
that he himself had put it there

to this day the stab wound keeps bleeding
not as bad now as before

but when it does stop oozing
my friend picks at the scab

and reaches for the language knife
just in case it's needed once again.

TIERRA AMARILLA

born from the side of a woman
like Cain and Abel

he struck a chord
in haste

the brown cat of Action Poetry
El Movimiento (place whiskers here)

how many poets answered the call
with a sword

or guns blazing sirens blaring
only Tijerina was not yellow

the rest of us took up the pen
or gave up

became teachers
the easy way out

or like so many
became the enemy

CON MAX

Max writes about death now
that's all he knows

bumping knees with moist caves
tree angels sink

driving the streets of Nixon
and Gonzales, Texas oh so long ago

a crest of his mama's furniture
teenage girls with big jugs (big jugs always in)

his new stories
romance a blonde sixty year old woman

or the splinter of a Mexican girl
in a Westside bar

his old Volkswagen Beetle
brought to life even in death

Culebra Street
still warm to the touch

EL PRESUMIDO

my dad made a grotto
out of cement

pa' que abuela could
put La Virgen de San Juan

in the front yard
by the double windows

con las flores moradas
their name eludes me now

la Virgen must have
done its job

because abuela lived to be
a hundred

hope La Virgen bears in mind
I was abuela's favorite

VENTANA

I followed the mangy dog
into a barrio

you could count the bones
of his ribs and shoulders

the sunken eyes
of its lost race

no illustrious ancestors
no hope to lick while waiting for tomorrow

children threw stones
at him

drunks kicked at him
old ladies yelled at him

with his tail between his legs
he saw his reflection in a storefront window

startled
I recognized myself

POEM WITH MEXICANS

I was buying my tacos
at La Joyita

when two Mexicans walked in,
one ordered tacos de lengua

"Quiero las tortillas tostaditas"
he told the girl behind the counter

the other one, the shorter one
got a Jarrito Morado

telling the taller one,
"Es bueno pa' la cruda"

good for the hangover he said
it was two in the afternoon

the sun
was taking a hammer to the sky

knocking birds to the ground
as if they were teeth

I got my tacos and left
being careful where I stepped

G-L-O-R-I-A

she came back from Iraq
with no legs

blown off by a roadside bomb
her best friend Celestino

lying in pieces
in and around the Humvee

Gloria had great thighs
in those volleyball shorts back in high school

her buttocks undulating so beautifully
as she jumped to block at the net

today in that same high school gym she smiles
sitting in her wheelchair in Army fatigues

while from a corner of her sweet mouth
a little sadness escapes onto the shiny floor

DESERT-LIKE PORTRAIT OF AGAPITO CÁRDENAS

my father's loneliness accumulates
by the Salton Sea

between mountains and desert
yet they do not stand a chance

my father overpowers them
in his black long sleeve shirt

the two top buttons open
he looks like a brown Cool Hand Luke

he grits his teeth on desert sand
having lost two wives

his son to the sky
loneliness surrounds him

the valley has become a funnel
and everything pours down upon his head

PROSE POEM POLQUITA

two black gangbangers
stole my rhyme

beige Hispanic punk took my parking spot
at a Paul Martínez Pompas reading

on the way there
a white racist shot my haiku

butch lesbian ripped off the poem
I wrote for my girl

damn cops planted a poem
from the evidence room in my hand

amigos, the poetry business is best left to those
who write prose

A LETTER TO CECILIO GARCÍA-CAMARILLO

Dear Cecilio,

In the years since you left us, there are so many things I wish I
could share with you, ask your opinions of this or that poem,
apologize to you for forgetting about La Raza, for neglecting the
hopes of carnalismo, for disrespecting las hermanas, for taking
poetry in so many wrong directions, for becoming an asshole, for
being a quitter sometimes. I don't know how you did it, always
so selfless, almost as if you yourself were the Other. I don't mean
to cry on your shoulder, but I miss you so much, carnal, brother,
mentor, hero, friend. I am trying to get back on the right road,
and asking your help.

Your faithful servant,
Reyes Cárdenas

MALCRIADO

When there was a death in the family,
grandma covered the mirror with a sheet,

told us boys we couldn't watch TV
for a thousand years,

said, don't turn on the radio either.
I questioned myself sarcastically,

can I scratch the sun's round ball,
can I look into the naked, virgin moon?

And sure enough when grandma went
to the wake or the funeral,

I'd turn on the TV
and keep a good eye on the driveway,

lest I be surprised—
Dios and God not being equal.

FOR CECILIO GARCÍA-CAMARILLO

I cannot stand your silence,
what you would have thought

of this or that hungry poet,
what New Mexican sky

would be enough for you,
what fine desert sand

you would welcome into your house,
what dark mountains you'd climb

(Aztlan perhaps just out of reach)
the sun blazing

in an Aztec dawn,
the enemy high-tailing it out of town,

you hot on their trail
to offer mercy.

BY THE TIME I GET TO PHOENIX

By the time I get to Phoenix
you'll be gone.

You'll be in handcuffs
leaving your American-born kids behind.

You left your green card at home
and you're on your way to Mexico.

By the time I make Albuquerque
you won't find a job across the border.

By the time I make Oklahoma
you'll be crossing that big desert.

By the time I get to Texas
I'll hear they've found your body.

SUNSHINE SUPERPAPI

Faster than a speeding bullet,
my father walked through Hiroshima.

The face of a child
like a melted Dali clock.

My father thought he was Superman
and tried to fly.

The sky's not made for Mexicans,
he finally figured out.

He gathered his cape around himself
and kept on walking.

A lone chimney stood like a phone booth,
my father thought he'd change.

SELF-CADENAZOS

They took me to the curandera
because I had TB.

She smeared some kind of manteca
on my John Keats chest.

My lungs got fat and sluggish.
The gringo doctor said uh oh.

He recommended pills and surgery.
Rodrigo, his gay male nurse, offered paperwork.

Beeswax in the ear, honey-stings in the eye,
could poetry save me from the saw?

My lungs (the two flat tortillas you see before you)
sucked in the air extraordinaire again.

I don't really know which brujas cured me,
or whose poetic career I wound up with.

EL AZTECA

You can't tell an Aztec
that there's more than one sun.

You can't tell him
that the sun and stars are one and the same.

You can't tell him
that the sun will die one day.

He's so fixated with the sun,
I don't know how he makes it through the night.

A MOTHER'S RESURRECTION

I start across the bridge
the rickety old bridge

which crosses Geronimo Creek
and leads to the cemetery

overgrown by weeds
where my mother has lain

for fifty years now
waiting patiently to be reborn

waiting for the wind to pick up
and the clouds to gather

the fresh spring rain to fall
upon her face

announcing that it's time to get up
and live again.

CIPRIANO "EL CIPPY" GÓMEZ

El Cippy was
the kind of vato

who'd drink
hot sauce through a straw

he was
the kind of vato

who'd start a fight
with a troop of Girl Scouts

he had a sharp
and insulting tongue

even when he was
complimenting barrio girls

and in a knife fight
with rival vatos

you could count
on El Cippy

being right behind you
sí never in front of you

MI TIERRA

Javier walked through the deserts
of Arizona in the night

looking for water
Toribio walked in the valley of Texas

drying off slowly
in the cold night

Mando jumped the fence
not far from Tijuana

and each of them is singing
this land is my land

from California
to the New York Island

MEXICAN METAMORPHOSIS

he woke up in the morning
and he was a jaguar

the pain of it
radiated out like the sun

dragged its claws
on the surface of the moon

its teeth
clamping down on stars

he tried
to escape his cage

he ran
to the ends of the earth

he was indeed
a jaguar

he growled
he felt his whiskers tremble

he lay down
in his own darkness

his eyes blinking
a wild and heavy wonder

CECILIO'S HOUSE

cecilio comes to me in a dream
and asks

if I will help him
paint his house

of course, amigo
I tell him

we paint all day
and all night

we paint for a week straight
we paint all month

I tell him
amigo, you sure have a big house

he says
reyes, the house of poetry is big

and I doubt
we'll ever finish painting it

YO TAMBIÉN CONOCÍ AL LOUIE

yo también conocí al louie
but he was not a friend of mine

he hung out
with a bad crowd

he was a hero
to them

I stayed out of their way
stuck to my books

papi, back from korea
insisted on it

I hung out
con mis primos

when they weren't
hanging out con el louie

and the rest
of his palomilla

whenever our eyes met
I could see

they hated me
maybe the cabrones admired me

the eyes
never lie said mama

on the night
que se chingaron al louie

I was
graduating from high school

still I felt
sorry for him and his vatos locos

MUST BE THE SEASON OF THE WITCH

made of flesh
and blood

I had my way
made

sixteen year old Antonia Rico
pregnant

hung out at the Royal Sports Hall
where Plácido Montemayor

stabbed my friend
Ramiro Chicasbolas you know where

on a night when
La Llorona failed to show

EL KING OF THE HOOD

he ruled the hood
with an iron fist

drug money
is honest money

he told his two year old
whose mother

he beat
to keep in line

he was the king
of the hood

until he met his fate
nel the cops

didn't shoot him
they sent him to the pen instead

ninety nine years
with no possibility of parole

slightly better
than the permanent hole

until someone did just that
put his lights out para siempre

with a can
of refried beans

swung inside a calcetín
a tube sock

is a mighty equalizer
wonder how he'll do in hell

SAN ANTONIO RIVER

the San Antonio River
is dirty

like Westside girls
making out

with dirty boys
late at night

in abandoned parks
panties halfway

down dark thighs
boys hurrying

along the trash-filled
San Antonio River

screaming their way
to the Gulf of Mexico

EL SONIDO MISTERIO

Doña Leonor was busy
trying to guess

El Sonido Misterio
on KCOR

rolling out fresh tortillas
for her no good son Refugio

who kept putting
his hands

in his pocket
to make sure

that the wad of bills
he robbed

from the convenience store
was still there

all twenty-two dollars of it
Doña Leonor

never did guess what
that sonido was

and kicked herself
when the winner

guessed that it was
fingernails scratching a washboard

CHUYITO LA RATA

allí por la calle Martín
Chuyito stole

an eight track player
from a car

the tape was of Steppenwolf
what kind of Mexican

listens to this cagada
on the Westside

said Chuyito to himself
he got rid of the player

the same way
he got rid of everything he stole

el Bigotón Pérez
reminded Chuyito

of a big fat Cantinflas
a pinche Steppenwolf tape

Chuyito scratched his head
as he shoved the money in his pocket

VEINTE DOCE

she asked
La Virgen de Guadalupe

for one little thing
under the brown clouds

by the swollen arroyo
a mangy ghostly dog

looking up
with borrowed eyes

she knew
La Virgen would provide

even here
in the distant future

POOR MEXICAN WOMAN

his mother was a plain
poor Mexican woman

so poor the fields
shied away from her

the cornstalks
shivered on hot windless days

the sun pretended
to be a cloud all day long

mice found nothing
in the barn

the arroyo stayed dry
even during downpours

he has no idea
how such a poor Mexican woman

could afford
to make him into a poet

FROM AZTLAN

TO THE MOONS of MARS

A CHICANO VERSE NOVELA 2010

THE FINAL FRONTIER INDEED, PIPORRO

Lupito had lost track
of how many trips

he'd made to Mars
or to the moons of Jupiter

whether helping move
scientific equipment

to study the Face on Mars
or volunteering on ships

harvesting methane
from one of the Jovian moons.

Of course he missed his wife
and kids back in Texas,

but with so few jobs
back on Earth

for a man his color
since the new edicts

became the law
of the land,

space had become
his only option.

THE COMPUTER WORE GUARACHES

"Rey, what the hell
is going on, hombre?"

said the skipper
in a nervous tone.

Rey was Rey Urías,
in charge of all

computer systems
on a derelict space freighter.

The ship had been in route
to the frozen moon of Jupiter.

The harvesting of ice
had become big business,

it had become
the only way to cool

the ever warming Earth
where temperatures

even at the poles
easily reached 130 degrees at night.

Yet, most conservatives
still denied

the existence
of global warming.

All Rey
would say about that was

"pinche pendejos...
tan bien bueyes..."

and those are the things
which are SFW,

in case
you're reading this at work.

THE NEW MARTIANS

Isidra's grandparents
had fled north

during the Mexican Revolution.
She had always considered herself

an American
first and foremost,

but the new edicts
had made her

a stranger in her own land.
She found

her life here on Mars
a welcome relief.

Studying the ancient
Martian civilizations

really put
"life" into perspective,

the racism
which was running rampant on Earth

meant little
if nothing

to her and her
fellow "New Martians,"

as the scientists
and technicians

jokingly
referred to each other.

OF LOVE-MAKING ON MARS

Isidra had not been
with Rey Urías,

her boyfriend,
in eighteen months,

what with him
being gone on round trips

to Earth
sixteen months at a time.

When they did
get together,

they made the most of it,
made love madly

and afterward, conversed…
sometimes it amazed her

how much just plain ordinary
face to face conversation could mean.

But soon, all too soon,
they both accepted the ache

they knew they would succumb to
when they parted again.

Out the portal
they could see

the endless red planet,
and sunset just a distant darkness.

EXPLORING THE FACE

Though the amazing technologies
found in the interiors

of the Face on Mars
were a rewarding

and astounding experience
no one yet knew

what the hell they were.
Isidra and her colleagues

could only catalog
and separate

and basically
just put things

into similar piles.
It would probably be decades

before they could even
venture an educated guess.

The Martians had evidently been
an exceedingly advanced civilization,

and to the New Martians,
the earthly Martians,

it was inconceivable
how such a great

and mighty civilization
could have become extinct.

Yet, what was going on back on Earth
maybe offered a clue.

As Isidra moved a panel
made of an exotic metallic foil,

a chill went up her spine
as she realized

that there,
on the wall,

was a representation
of the Pyramid of the Sun.

EL GRITO

Dolores del Grito
was a compiler,

she used unimaginable
computer languages

to catalog and condense
into understandable human terms,

things that would otherwise
boggle the mind.

Speaking of that,
she was having a little trouble herself —

concentrating had become
quite a task lately,

since she kept thinking of sex.
She missed Juanito,

damn chaparrito was off to the moons
of Jupiter again.

This business of satisfying herself
was not working anymore.

She had half a mind
of asking Isidra

if she could "borrow" Rey
next time his ship

made a pit stop.
But she was embarrassed to ask

even though it was something
which was accepted,

since there were more women
than men

on this godforsaken corner
of the solar system.

Is there really a sun,
or is it just an ancient rumor,

she asked herself
as she crunched

more numbers
into the stupid computer.

"Shinelas, Dolores, get aholt of yourself,"
she heard herself say out loud.

Debbie Rodgers, another compiler,
smiled curiously at herself,

and kept on pecking
like a chicken at her keyboard.

COLLISION WITH TIME

The S.S. Denham Dentifrice
was still drifting in space.

Rey Urías and his techs
had been awake twenty-six hours now,

trying to figure out
what had gone wrong

with all shipboard computers.
Black coffee

was not working anymore,
some idiot tech

was passing around toothpicks
as a joke.

Rey was about
to reprimand him

when there was a loud explosion,
the whole ship shuddered,

it felt like it was
going to break apart.

They had been dangerously close
to one of the outer rings of Saturn,

perhaps they had drifted
into the path of a shepherding moon.

Rey rushed to a portal,
looked out,

and to his horror,
saw a huge debris field.

He checked the pressure,
to his relief

pressure was normal.
He scratched his head,

what the hell did we hit?
Just then

Captain Juárez called him
to the bridge.

The Captain said,
incredulously

"How in God's name
did HAL get here?" (not really what he said)

A sickening, mechanical voice
uttered matter of fact over the ship's intercom,

"The stories of my demise
have been greatly exaggerated.

I bow
to no man!"

MAY THE FORCE BE WITH YOU, REY URÍAS

Isidra felt
a disturbance in the force,

as if a million people
had just died,

or was it just gas,
maybe she was pregnant,

oh, hell no!
She grabbed her stomach.

A few minutes later
she got the news

that Rey had been
in an accident,

but was ok,
thank God he was ok.

She lit a candle
to La Virgen de Guadalupe,

she felt like strangling him
or shoving him

into a swollen arroyo,
but soon she regained her senses,

went back to work.
Perhaps

the angry red planet
had not been a misnomer.

Having a hard time
trying to go to sleep that night,

she kept remembering
their last goodbye,

he'd said, "here's looking
at you, Prieta,"

as he kissed her.
He had such a way with words.

HAL 9000

Rey and his techs,
nine women and two men,

were finally able
to pinpoint the computer problems,

they got the system
running at ninety percent.

Captain Chon Juárez
was pleased,

(some of the crew called him Capitán Chones
behind his back, of course)

he was too busy
to compliment anyone,

since he was
still trying to assess the damage.

A few hours later,
it turned out to be

minimal damage.
The object they had collided with

turned out to be
a thousand year old relic.

A hundred years ago
another ship had taken

a glancing blow
from this so-called HAL 9000 chingadera.

The Capitán wanted to send
a demolition team

to blow it up.
The S.S. Denham Dentifrice

was not allowed to carry weapons,
but it was transporting

mining explosives.
He finally thought better of it,

continued on to Ganymede,
the decision gnawing at his insides.

Meanwhile, Rey Urías slept well that night,
and dreamed of Debbie Rodgers.

PLANETA DE LA DEBBIE

Debbie Rodgers
was a natural at her job,

often figuring out artifacts
before workers with more experience

even had a clue.
Debbie was too well-endowed —

if there is such a thing
to a man.

Every time Rey set foot
on Mars,

he'd rush to Isidra's workplace,
not so much to see her,

but to sneak
lascivious glances at Debbie.

He had the hots for her
and took it out on Isidra,

who was flattered
by his passionate love-making,

unaware Rey's mind
dwelled on another heavenly body.

Rey never felt any guilt.
What man does?

The space between a man's ears
more vast than outer space.

CAT FIGHT

Isidra and Rey made love.
But if the earth moved,

Earth was too far away to tell.
Isidra woke up

from a fitful yet lusty sleep.
Rey was still far off

on the other side of Jupiter,
but at least he was ok.

Isidra distracted herself
with work.

She had not told anyone else
about that representation

of the Pyramid of the Sun she'd found.
Were we in fact Martians,

had Martians created
our earthly civilizations?

That certainly
would piss off the Creationists

who now ruled Earth,
insisting that Earth was only

six or eight days old.
Isidra forgot

what other pendejadas
those tarugos advocated.

When Isidra walked into the office
in the morning

the first thing
she saw was Debbie,

wearing
a sheer top,

leaving nothing
to the imagination,

not that Isidra
gave a damn,

she just didn't like
Debbie flaunting

her numerous attributes
when Rey was around.

It made her very jealous
when he stared at that little chichona.

As soon as her mind
uttered those vicious thoughts,

she felt guilty.
The heart is, indeed, a lonely hunter.

EXILE ON A MARTIAN STREET

If you're not a home run hitter,
you bunt, thought Debbie

in the ancient terminology
her grandfather had taught her.

Normally only Mexicans
ended up here

on the outer solar system,
cast out by her race —

the white race,
which she was not

so fond of,
but accepted it

as a foregone conclusion.
So how had a white girl

become self-exiled?
She often wondered.

"Debbie, Debbie,"
Isidra had been trying

to get Debbie's attention.
"Debbie, I'm going

to get a bite to eat,
do you want to join me?"

Out the portals,
the Martian winds

were blowing
red dirt around like snow.

Marvin was twittering,
wearing crazy goggles,

his green hands on the plunger
ready to blow up the Eoit.

HIS VORPAL SWORD

Rey Urías took
his vorpal sword in hand

and ripped off Debbie's clothes
neatly piling them on the floor,

panties on top,
bra cups rising like desire.

That's all he remembered
of the dream

as the ship headed
back to Mars for repairs.

Captain Chon
had indeed gotten his way

and had
HAL 9000 blown to smithereens.

Wonder what the jonesthereens,
think about that,

chuckled Rey Urías
as he took the elevator

up to the bridge
where Captain Chon

was barking orders
like a dog.

The second in command
appeared neutered

as he kept saluting
and crying, "Yes, sir, yes, sir,

yes, sir!"
ad nauseam.

When the Captain finished his ejaculations,
Rey said,

"Hey, Chon,
what's our ETA to Mars?"

A million miles away,
the angry red planet

did not appear
so angry or so red

as it staggered and stumbled
in its orbit.

JANUS

Underneath the face of Mars
the caverns were deep and dark,

the structure shifted
and bits of red dust

fell from the ceilings
to enter Isidra's lungs

through her dust mask.
The artificial atmosphere

would only do so much
down there.

She uncovered the replica
(or was it the original?)

of the Pyramid of the Sun.
Questions and anxiety

filled her scientific mind again.
Such possibilities,

such unfathomable things
spanked her naked mind

which was suddenly emptied
by someone's voice echoing behind her.

She quickly covered
the replica.

It was Dolores,
and she appeared in pain.

Dolores hated descending
the countless stairs and ladders,

but she insisted on wearing
her high heeled shoes everywhere she went.

Isidra glared
at la pendeja.

THE ROYAL

After la pendeja
had left,

climbing the ladders
exposing her ample backside,

Isidra quietly removed
the red alloy screws

which held the replica
in place.

She was startled to find
Martian writing

where she had removed the replica.
Even more startling

were the three embossed buttons.
Isidra had not mastered

the Martian language
but she knew enough

to read
the instructions

underneath the buttons.
She pressed them

in the sequence
called for,

sixty-nine positions in all.
A door silently opened.

She almost passed out,
her heart was racing.

The tomb of a Martian royal
glowed with a hum.

DOWN UNDER

Isidra made notes
of every step

she had taken
to access the chamber.

Her boss, Eulogio "Chuniar" Luna, Jr.
was a stickler for protocol.

Facts were not facts
until he said they were facts.

Isidra often thought
the son of a bitch

made his mother
provide proof she was his mother.

The Martian's skin still looked good
considering it was at least

a hundred thousand years old.
She tapped notes

on her Lalo5.
A Lalo5 is a ring-size computer,

they come in all colors.
Isidra's was brown, of course,

as any proud New Martian
would insist upon.

Once she was back
on the surface,

she looked up at the sky
to see Deimos and Phobos

scatter into the night
like fireflies.

Yes, a large number of New Martians
are descendants of the Arizona Mexicans

who were rounded up and sent to the
penal colony that once made up Mars.

STIRRINGS IN THE DARK

While Isidra
ate her supper,

down in the bowels
of the Face on Mars

silence struggled
with silence —

as silence
is wont to do,

and dust clung to dust,
photons became even prouder.

In the sepulchre
a muscle or two twitched,

a leg and arm
tried to return to warmth,

realized heat as something good,
became slowly accustomed to it.

Funny how a hundred thousand years
can be wiped away

with the blink of an eye.
Darkness was his light,

he relished
in its presence.

He recognized
his own life.

THE END OF THE WORLD AS THEY KNEW IT

He was the last ruler
to finish his reign

before the giant comet
appeared beyond the Ort Cloud.

Soon the royal astronomers
had confirmed

that all would be lost
if something wasn't done.

But all attempts to re-direct
the giant icy rock failed.

After the ruler's descension
and enshrinement,

Martian civilization survived
another fifty years

before the atmosphere was destroyed
by the inevitable impact.

A cloud of red dust rose into space
like a beautiful intergalactic flower,

and flourished there
for a million years.

LA ROSA DE TEJAS

Juanito had been missing
Dolores del Grito.

After ten months
harvesting the moons of Jupiter

he was ready
to head back home to Mars.

His space freighter, La Rosa de Tejas,
was full to the brim

with purple methane
and rock ice.

The processing plants on Mars
would process the raw materials

and ship them back to Earth,
to the gringo world,

where only pure-bred white people
were allowed to live —

with a few minor exceptions.
The last Mexicans on Earth

are being deported to the moon
as we speak.

THE ROUNDUP

> *"The ground on which the ball bounces*
> *Is another bouncing ball."*
> Delmore Schwartz

Meanwhile, back on Earth,
Lupito's wife, Chela,

and Lupito's two kids
are being herded into spaceships

for their trip
to the moon.

When these ten spaceships
leave Earth,

there will be no more Mexicans
left on the planet.

From the moon,
they will be transported to Mars.

Chela calls Lupito
on the aluristo,

a sort of telephone device
which carries voice across space

at a hundred thousand times
the speed of light.

"Lupito, me and the kids
are on the way to the moon."

"Good, Chela, I can't wait
to see y'all,

I'll be anxiously awaiting
your arrival, amor."

The silent rocket ship motors
barely made a noise

as the spacecraft
slid along clouds momentarily

before it reached
the blackness of space.

MOONWALKING MEXICANS

Chela and her kids,
Lupito Jr. and Griselda Marie,

were housed
in bracero-type barracks

while they awaited
their transfer to Mars.

Despite all the technological advances,
the trip to Mars

would still take
at least eight months,

depending on
cargo priorities.

Lupito Jr. and Griselda
enjoyed playing

on the moon
with the other kids.

They had never been able
to jump so high,

throw a ball so far.
They rolled down craters

not heeding the warnings
to be careful with their space suits.

"Chamacos will be chamacos,
I guess," said Chela.

PEPE

Lupito threw moonrocks
for Pepe (his dog) to fetch.

Of course, Pepe
had to use

the mechanical mouth
which was part of his space suit

to fetch
the tasteless moon rocks,

so it took most
of the fun out of it

and soon Pepe was doggone bored.
Lupito and Griselda

bounced a hundred feet
into the airless air

as they headed
back inside.

Being kids
they were not

impressed at all
as the racist blue and white

ball of earth
slid silently into view.

Pepe tried his best
to mark his territory,

but only succeeded
in marking his space suit.

DOGS ARE SHAKESPEAREAN, CHILDREN ARE STRANGERS IN A STRANGE LAND

Meanwhile, back on Earth,
Speedy Gonzales ran for his life.

The Sheriff was pissed
that one dirty Mexican was still at large,

and roaming Arizona freely
which by God-given right

belonged to white people only.
But Speedy, true to his name,

was impossible to catch,
making fools of Arpaio's ghouls,

running circles around them
while shouting,

"Arriba! Arriba!"
pointing to Pepe

up on the lunatic moon.
"Arriba! Arriba!"

shouted
Speedy Gonzales.

THE RETURN

As the S.S. Denham Dentifrice
returned to Mars from the dark side

and swung around
to the daylight side,

those who happened
to be looking out the portals

were astounded
that the Face on Mars

was lit up a bright,
blinding red.

The Captain immediately
called Mars Control

inquiring about
the strange phenomenon.

The reply was:
they are investigating it now.

Rey had been
taking a nap,

dreaming either of
Isidra or Debbie,

what's the difference
he thought to himself,

a woman
is a woman,

interchangeable,
malleable,

always gullible
to the right man.

Rey had never been known
for his political correctness.

That's what a macho
is all about, after all,

he insisted
to his alter ego.

ONE MAN SHORT

The structure was immense
(and tense),

it could be seen
by distant spaceships.

Isidra and her team
had rushed to investigate,

only to be attacked
by the ancient Martian

as they entered
the blazing hallways of light—

hallways which had always
been dark until now.

The team's artificial lighting
had never been sufficient

for anthropological research.
Beto, the young intern,

(he was twenty or so)
was cut in half by the Martian

with a mere, meticulous look.
Everyone ran for cover,

shaking and horrified.
Isidra yelled,

"Go! Go!" meaning
haul ass outta here.

They scrambled to the surface
one man short.

Isidra cried
bulbous tears.

RED LIGHT DISTRICT

After Isidra gathered
her senses,

she called her boss.
He in turn

called the security chief
who initiated

evacuations to the shelters.
There was no police force

on Mars,
not what one normally associates

with police —
no weapons whatsoever

were allowed
except for those

the whites flooded
Earth and the Earth's moon with.

The only thing resembling weapons
on Mars was explosives used

for mining the moons
of Jupiter and Saturn.

How this monster
was going to be stopped

was beyond anybody's
comprehension.

Isidra nursed
her mental wounds,

feeling responsible
for Beto's death.

She thought
about the Martian,

what have we
gotten ourselves into

she thought pensively out loud
to herself or to anybody who would listen

as the Face on Mars flashed its red
sickening light about.

POZO LIBRE

Isidra feels like La Llorona,
having drowned her child

in the waters of this Martian monster.
A monster which she herself had discovered,

thought of it as something amazing,
a wonder to behold,

which had now
come out of its

centuries old sleep
only to kill. To kill.

The Martian had not
followed them to the surface.

What's it waiting for,
she wondered

in the space of her space suit,
the cold winds of Mars

kicking up ice dust
onto her visor

just at the moment
Rey Urías had teleported

to the surface.
She wondered

if it was too soon
for him to have heard the news.

Even though her boss
had specifically told her

to head back to the relative safety of campus,
she decided

to go back down
into the abyss.

THE TELEPORTING BLUES

"The Mexican will always be
a caged animal,

though he tries to be good
it is not within his nature,

he cheats, he scams,
he lies,

and this comes easy to him.
He excels in it,

he glories in it,
ay dios mio,

in this the pendejo
is unsurpassed."

Every damn time he teleported,
these kinds of thoughts

filled the mind of Rey Urías
and always left him

uneasy, afraid of himself.
Somehow or other,

Rey always convinced himself
that he was a good Mexican,

contrary to
the evidence.

RING-A-DING-DING

Aboard the S.S. César Chávez,
Lupito busied himself with work.

After he had talked
to Chela and the kids,

Lupito and the other workers
continued harvesting

the rings of Saturn.
After a year

of harvesting the rings,
there were only two rings left.

In six months,
the work would be done,

and they would move on
to the rings of Neptune.

It was a dirty job,
but someone had to do it.

THERE'S GOLD IN DEM DAR PLANETS

Planetary rings usually consist
of two percent gold,

in the solar economy,
that's worth

all the effort
the New Martians put into it.

Since Earth
is off limits to Mexicans now,

this gold trading
becomes sweet revenge.

The gringos back on Earth
pay a heavy price

for this extra-planetary gold.
These traficantes of ring gold

look at this trafficking
as poetic justice —

minus the poetry,
of course,

and, maybe,
even, minus the justice.

IN DANTE'S INFERNO

Isidra descended into
the bright, red hallways,

cautiously, ever so cautiously.
She had removed her shoes,

the heels of her feet
barely touched the stone surface.

If she came face to face
with the Martian monster,

she had no plan.
What her urgent intentions were—

she had no clue.
She felt she owed it to Beto

to, at least, get his personal belongings
off his severed body

while at the same time hoping
not to meet the same fate.

Beto's torso lay against a wall,
her heart pounding against

her small breasts.
She reached into his pockets,

she unclipped his I.D. badge,
she struggled to pull a ring

from a white, lifeless finger.
A noise startled her,

it was just a fine dust
falling from the ceiling above her.

She hurried out,
hallway after endless hallway.

When she reached the surface,
her eyes were still seeing red,

the red of those lights down there
made her stomach upset.

She felt queasy.
She threw up.

WASSUP, MY MIGAS!

After a hearty breakfast of migas,
Rey Urías decided he'd walk

over to the lab
to see Isidra.

When he got there
he found out

that Isidra was among
the missing.

Why had no one bothered
to tell him?

He rounded up
a couple of his techs,

Rufino and Modesta,
to accompany him

to the pyramid
(which is what most New Martians called

the complex known
as the Face on Mars).

They approached carefully
from the side

which was bathed in shadows.
They, of course, had no weapons,

not even their cunning, just the aluristos
for communication.

What good communication
would do them

was something
they chose to ignore.

Suddenly Isidra
came out of nowhere.

Shortly, they had
to change their shorts,

not literally, of course,
pero ya mero.

Isidra grabbed Rey
and hugged the hell out of him.

She hugged him so damn hard
he almost let go a miga pedo.

Out here on desolate Mars,
in a space suit, hell, that could be deadly.

She told him about Beto.
Rey did not know Beto that well

but he felt bad for Isidra.
They hurried back

to the relative safety
of the lab

passing the rusty, robotic spirit
of an antique, Martian probe,

there was no opportunity
for the weary to stop and rest.

THE ABOMINATION

After a hundred thousand years
of sleep,

waking up to this confusion,
the Martian

tried her best
to regain her senses.

There were questions
in her mind,

but not such things
as we would know as questions.

Who were these creatures
in her sanctity?

Why did they befoul it
with their presence?

Didn't they know
the Great Forbidden Laws?

She must,
if it remained within her power,

wipe them all out.
She must prepare herself

to walk upon her planet,
her planet,

reclaim her homeland.
She did not know

how many of these abominations
were out there

(she was thinking like a gringa
on Fox News).

She must go to the surface
and face them.

EVE OF DESTRUCTION

The Security Council
ordered Captain Chon Juárez

to bring whatever explosives
were left on the ship

to the surface of Mars,
and ándale pronto.

The Council had decided
that dynamite

was their only form
of defense.

No one was sure
that it would work at all,

but that was their only hope.
Rey told anyone who would listen

that he did not think
the Martian would leave

the safety of its sanctuary.
But even as Rey spoke,

the Martian took her first steps
towards the surface.

SINE=TPACE

Basking in the three hundred degree
below zero temperature,

she relished the sweet
Martian atmosphere,

her belt-shaped lung caressed
each molecule of red dust,

her minds full of questions,
questions not framed like ours,

questions which protruded
into space,

questions which could knock
moons from their

comfortable, but silly orbits.
Man's creation of mathematics

was revealed to be
a pure, stupid, invention,

thus making time and space
quite impossible.

She was driven
by the survival of her race,

unaware she was
the last of her kind.

She sensed the creatures
had retreated

to those strange structures.
She no longer felt

threatened by them.
But, her twenty,

separate minds
urged dangerous caution.

EL PLAN ESPIRITUAL DE MARTE

The plan
was to attack the Martian

if it attempted to come
through the entryway of the lab.

Its colossal hallway
would serve as a trap.

The explosives would be placed
in a way

which would cause
no damage to the entryway,

but, yet, would hopefully
destroy the Martian.

Rey and Isidra
retreated to her quarters

until the Martian
made its approach, if it did.

Isidra's panties lay
on Rey's pants,

which he'd flung
to the floor.

Isidra did not
remove her bra

during their lovemaking.
(Gente, this is the point

in the narrative
where the proverbial train

enters the tunnel of love).
Meanwhile, the Security Council

kept a vigil
on the security cameras

for any sign
of the Martian.

By this time, the Martian's minds
had been made up.

Her emotions
gathered in one place.

CAPITÁN COPASLLENAS

The S.S. Gloria Anzaldúa
had been hurtling toward Mars

when it heard about
the terrifying occurrence,

and was now
in stationary orbit

above the lab complex.
It had a load

of explosives
headed to the mining camps

on the moons of Jupiter.
Captain Lola Copasllenas

had burned a lot of uranium
on this accelerated trip.

She beamed down
the explosives as instructed

and awaited
further orders.

Lola was young,
and had been

promoted to Captain
when she was only twenty-three.

Now at twenty-eight
she was a veteran

out here on the outskirts
of the solar system.

She was the only lesbian
of the eleven female captains

making up the Mexican space fleet
of nineteen starships,

ships which were
way beyond their prime —

and with nothing akin
to the stars.

GRINGOLANGOS

Mexico City looked ridiculous,
inhabited as it was

by the white people
repatriated from Arizona.

Every damn Mexican had been
exiled to the moon,

and then on to Mars.
Well, not every Mexican —

the Native Mexican Indians
had been considered

not worth the trouble
so they were just given

a "vaccine" which immediately
put them out of their misery.

Back on Mars,
every contingency

had been addressed.
No one in the lab

knew if the Martian
would stay underground

or come knocking
on the impenetrable door.

A door made on Ganymede
of unobtainium

which had somehow been obtained
by the stubborn, sweaty cojones

of the men
and women miners

with the loss
of many space-suited vidas locas.

THE DOOR OF PERCEPTION

When the security cameras failed,
the Council asked for volunteers

to go check the cameras
since the problem appeared to be

with the equipment itself,
and not with the computer controls

or the software.
Rey volunteered

together with two other
techs.

They were working
on the cameras

when the impenetrable door
was ripped apart

and flung hundreds
of yards away

into a nearby crater.
The dust rose

and settled quickly.
The three volunteers

were staring into the Martian's
flaming, red lips,

emotions clearly visible
in the Martian's square eyes,

eyebrows which covered
and uncovered her eyes.

Suddenly, it lashed out
at Mariano,

he fell dead without a sound.
Beatriz did not even

have a chance
to express terror on her beautiful face

before her beautiful face
lay in shreds.

THE GREAT ESCAPE

Rey had no idea
how he had managed

to crawl into the vent
which routed cables

and wires from who knew where.
He remained quiet,

afraid the Martian
could hear him.

After an hour,
he decided to follow the vent

wherever it might lead,
preferably to safety.

Indeed, the vent
led to the library.

He kicked out the vent guard,
jumped down

and hurried to
the control center.

The Council members
were still in shock,

and considering
their next move.

Apparently Rey
and the techs

had fixed the
security cameras

just before
they were attacked.

The Martian was sitting
with her back against a wall.

She seemed at peace,
but inside of her,

methane words
were being

put together
and taken apart

for a purpose
which was not evident

on the monitors
in the control room.

RAZA CÓSMICA

The Martian,
unaware of its mejicanidad,

has horrible dreams
of jaguars

as it sleeps
against a wall,

pyramids startle her
into a deeper sleep,

her haven,
her long sleep

inside the Face
has blown wide open

as if a hurtling rock
from space has demanded space.

Where do these creatures
come from,

from what wayward moons?
She cannot see

her connections to them.
She does not know

they are
her descendants.

PURA LECHE

Isidra had been
in her quarters

when the attack
on the lab occurred.

She called Rey
on his aluristo.

No answer.
She called a friend

on the Council.
They told her

Rey was ok,
but that Beatriz

and Mariano
had been killed.

She felt so bad,
yet so happy

that Rey was alive, and she was
overwhelmed by guilty pleasure.

Octavio Paws
was purring at her feet.

She gave him
a bowl of milk.

"Why can't Mexicans
have nine lives?" Isidra cried.

She turned the bra cups
to the front.

She wanted to go
to the cafeteria

and look outside,
but of course

the titanium shutters
had been rolled down.

"Hell, it's the same old
angry red planet,"

she said out loud
as she bent over

to pet Octavio Paws,
who was embroiled

in his own labyrinth
of milk mustaches.

THE THING

One second the security cameras
showed the Martian

resting peacefully
against the wall

of the entry way,
next second she was gone,

"poof," like an
Oliver de la Paz poem.

The Martian was
nowhere, man.

Suddenly, she was standing,
standing arms akimbo right there,

facing the Security Council
members,

stood there motionless,
fear and terror

gripping the council members,
(contrary to popular belief,

fear and terror
are not the same thing.

Fear, apparently,
has one more electron

than terror,
though most of us

would have bet
our Arizona beachfront properties

that it was terror
which had the extra electron).

Actually, the council members
were frozen stiff, dead stiff,

since the Martian's
intrusion into the chambers

had allowed the
three hundred below zero temps

on Mars
to enter unimpeded.

The emergency system
had closed all air-tight doors,

but there were
no doors

where the Martian
had broken thru.

THE BEST LAID PLANS OF MICE AND MEXIKANS

Luckily for the
Mexicans on Mars

most of the main
communities

were located on the
other side of the planet.

Still, the lab
was a sitting duck

for the Martian.
As Isidra watched

on the security cameras,
the Martian

inadvertently killed
the council members.

A proverbial light bulb
went off in Isidra's head.

She remembered the pristine
material that the Martian's

sarcophagus
or sepulchre was made of,

or whatever the hell
the Martian's resting place was called.

She remembered
that the technicians

had said
it was impenetrable.

She thought,
if we can reproduce

this material
maybe we can confine

the Martian
until we can

figure out
what to do with it.

FLOR SILVESTRE

She called Rey
on her aluristo

and told him
to meet her

at the Face on Mars
complex.

She gathered
six scientists

and explained
her plan to them.

They seemed skeptical,
but what else

could they do?
Death was not an option.

They worked diligently,
but always alert

to the fear that the Martian
would return to her lair.

For three days
they analyzed the material.

It turned out
to be organic.

They all
looked at each other

in amazement.
"Yes, yes,

we can reproduce this,"
Isidra smiled at Rey.

"How quickly?"
asked Rey.

Pronto, muy pronto,
said Isidra,

the echo
in her earpiece

brought her
back to stark reality.

AZTEC SACRIFICE

Isidra figured
that the Martian

had not been able
to escape its sarcophagus

for a hundred million years
except with the aid

of Isidra's own
tempering,

maybe they could
somehow get the Martian

back into its sarcophagus.
It was worth a shot heard 'round Mars.

That way they could
forego

trying to make
a sarcophagic replica

back at the lab,
since no one knew

what the Martian
would do next.

But, how would they get
the Martian back

down into the Face?
There would have to be

some kind of Aztec sacrifice.
You know,

in these situations
someone's always gotta die.

Chico, little did they know
that the Martian

was, even now,
(as I make this up)

already heading
towards the Face on Mars.

IT'S A DOG EAT DOG WORLD

Chela and the kids
boarded the last train

to Clarksville,
no, no, pendejos,

(the things
I call myself!),

actually, they boarded
the U.S.S. Ricardo Sánchez,

which was carrying
the last load of Mexicans

from the Earth's moon
to their future homeland

on Mars.
The kids followed Pepe the dog

around with
a pooper scooper.

Pepe looked out
every window

of the spaceship.
He wagged his tail,

and the dizzy fleas.
The Earth's blue marble

meant nothing to him.
White people

did not mean anything
to him.

He did not understand
the word racism.

He thought everybody
and everything was just another dog.

HACIENDO CARAS

While you guys were twittering
or haciendo caras

on Facebook,
the Mexicans on Mars

were busy concocting
a plan

to get rid
of the Martian

once and for all.
As luck would have it,

the S.S. Gloria Anzaldúa
commanded by Lola Copasllenas

was in stationary orbit
a hundred and sixty miles

above the Face on Mars,
and it would play

a vital part
in Isidra's plan

which had gone off
in her head

like a lightbulb,
or an orgasm.

The Martian herself,
unbeknownst to her,

was lending
a helping hand.

She was making
a beeline for the Face,

her multiple minds churning
like an asteroid belt.

Discarded Lady Gaga costumes
seemingly choking

each and every
spiky neuron in her thighs.

AND I HAVE MILES TO GO BEFORE I SLEEP

The Martian was tired
after all the exertion

of trekking to the lab and back.
It did not understand

these strangers.
They did not appear

to fear her,
she could not understand

how they stood there
motionless. (Pendeja, they're dead!)

But right now
she must get back

to her sanctuary.
She must rest.

Her body was screaming
for rest,

her minds
were not thinking clearly.

She must lie down.
She descended redly

to what she thought
would be

the safety
of her lair.

POWER OUTAGE

Isidra and Rey and
the others

had heard
the Martian's hollow footsteps,

her breathing,
they could almost hear

her heartbeat.
They hid in the shadows,

they adjusted the controls
on their space suits

so that the exhalators
(which recycled air)

kept the rushing air noise
to a minimum.

The Martian lay down
in its sarcophagus.

She seemed to fall
into a deep, cold sleep.

Rey and the strongest
of the technicians

pushed the lid
until they had

sealed the Martian
in her bed.

They hoped
to use the crane

to get the trapped Martian
to the surface.

Halfway up
with their Martian cargo,

the damn power went out.
Isidra used

her aluristo
to hurriedly call the lab.

"Power is out
all over the planet!"

was the response.
"You'd think

we were back in Méjico!"
said Isidra, hechando madres.

Maintaining reliable power
had always been a problem

even for the original
gringo scientists.

The angry red planet
could be a cabrón.

LOS REAL BURROS OF THE MARTIAN HILLS

"I have a plan, babe,"
Rey told Isidra.

"Call the lab,
have them send over

a couple of jackasses,
a couple of burros."

It took
about three hours,

but soon the burros
were hooked up

to the sarcophagus.
"Ándale, ándale!"

Rey yelled
at the burros

as he whipped
their space-suited asses

with a stone-tipped Mariachi belt.
The burros

seemed to look
at each other

and hee-hawed
"Who the hell

does this culero
think he is?"

After much labor,
the sarcophagus

reached the red surface.
Now to see if

the plan
would work.

Isidra's nervous smile
was reflected

against the shield
of her helmet.

WHERE NO MEXICAN HAS GONE BEFORE

The plan was to
beam the Martian

aboard the S.S. Gloria Anzaldúa
and beam it down

to Phobos—the ancient Martian
artificial satellite which had no

natural resources.
Lola Copasllenas

had volunteered
for the dangerous mission position.

Lupito also volunteered,
as well as Rey and Isidra.

The ship would have
to be operated

by a small crew,
(as luck would have it

Mexicans are already small)
in case the Martian

woke up
in a bad mood.

You movie-goers
know what an alien

can do
when let loose

on a spaceship.
No, you Tea Party bozos,

we're not talking
about illegal aliens.

Don't you cagados
remember

you sent us packing
to Mars?

Once the Martian
was beamed aboard,

the S.S. Anzaldúa
headed out on impulse power.

The brave crew felt
as if an asteroid belt

was tightening pecs
around their necks.

FLOR Y CANTO

As soon as they
pulled away from Mars,

Rey called everybody together
on the bridge.

"Camaradas, I have
an idea I want

to put before you."
Everyone looked quizzically at Rey

as he elaborated.
"Instead of taking

the Martian to Phobos,
I propose that

we take our Martian friend
to Earth."

Everyone's eyes opened wide
with surprise,

and smiles broke out
contagious

and pleasantly cruel
almost.

Soon everyone was cheering
and agreeing

that this indeed
should be done.

Lola Copasllenas
told her navigator,

"Set course for Earth,"
she ordered

Corporal Juan Phil Felipe.
"Right away, comandante!"

as he saluted
and punched the numbers

into the computer.
"Warp speed, comandante?"

"Yes, corporal, warp speed,"
said Copasllenas.

The star field
looked like a Flor y Canto.

WE BE TRIPPIN'

Once it was decided
to deliver the Martian to Earth,

excitement raged
among the crew.

Do not believe
what they say

about the emptiness
of space.

Space, amigos,
is full of space.

Don't laugh
until you've experienced

it yourself.
The plan

was to go
into stealth mode

once they got
close to Earth

so as not
to alert Earth's defenses.

Once in orbit
they would beam down

the Martian
to Washington D.C.

Casually, during breakfast,
Captain Copasllenas

asked nonchalantly,
(Chale, I didn't

just use the word "nonchalantly,"
did I?)

"I hope this mission
does not bother my conscience,"

said Copasllenas as she poked at her migas
with a piece of tortilla.

"After what
those people,

and I use
the word liberally,

after what
those people

have done
to the Mexican race,

I will not lose
any sleep over it!"

said Isidra
as they sped

at warp speed
towards the blue

and white marble
which had

once been
their home.

CHEECH AND CHONG'S NICE DREAMS

The Martian slept
peacefully,

unaware
it would take part

in Moctezuma's Revenge.
(No shit!)

The Martian dreamt
beautiful dreams —

for the moons of Mars
always have that effect,

even on non-Martians.
The hum

of the ship's motors
was loud

in the cargo hold.
The darkness and cold

exchanged molecules
like wedding vows.

The Martian stirred
and unstirred.

Earth's moon
almost head-on.

The S.S. Gloria Anzaldúa
rattles imperceptibly

as it slows down
into solid space.

BEAM ME DOWN, SCOTTY

The operation
had to be precise,

there could be
no screw-up,

Rey warned everyone.
The moment was at hand,

everything depended
on split-second timing,

it was like splitting hairs
or building

the Pyramid of the Sun
on the head of a needle.

The lid slid off
the sarcophagus

as the crew
pushed with all their might.

Transporter tech
Ensign Eddie Corral

was sweating profusely
as he stood by

the transporter levers.
Suddenly he plunged

the levers forward
to beam the Martian

down to D.C., (¡ahí les va, cabrones!)
a poetically justified smile

swept over his face
and over the face

of the others.
Mission accomplished, pal.

With high fives
all over the place,

they tossed
their space sombreros

into the manufactured air
of the S.S. Anzaldúa.

Cacophonous alarms
startled everyone

back to reality.
Missiles were approaching.

EYES WIDE OPEN

The deafly silence
was broken only

by the sound of cicadas
in Rey's head

as he looked
at Copasllenas

who was already
shouting orders.

"Double-shields up,
Double-shields up!"

she shouted
her orders quietly.

"Warp speed
as soon as possible."

She continued
as huge explosions

rocked
the S. S. Anzaldúa.

Outside, interstellar dust
became conscious,

woken out of its
billion years of sleep.

Everybody strapped
into their seats.

Suddenly they were
up to warp speed.

No looking back now, ese.
Copasllenas was checking

all aboard computers to see
(are there offboard computers?)

if there was any damage.
A gaseous plume

trailed the ship.
Back on Earth,

the Martian was coming out
of her Sertapedic sleep.

The Lincoln Monument
stared at her.

Was the race
of the Great Shemancipator

done for?
The Martian opened her eyes wide.

GOOGLE THIS

Limping home,
the crew was exhausted

while back on Mars,
the Mexicans

were partying into the dawn
proclaiming Copasllenas

and the rest
heroes.

Communication packets
were arriving

sporadically.
The Martian had gone

on a tear,
killing everyone in sight,

men women children
frogs bears

even destroying (for unknown reasons)
McDonald's Restaurants.

Whitey was
being wiped out

left and right, burro y elefante.
No actual reportage

was being done
by white humans.

No, indeed,
the only news

reaching Mars
and the S.S. Anzaldúa

was via
Google Robotic Reporters

which had taken over
news reporting

for the last
twenty years on Earth.

Some Google Robots
were reporting

that they too
were being attacked.

More news after
this message from our sponsor.

Google,
The Super Raza search engine.

BRAVE NEW CHANTE

The crippled ship
arrived at Mars

todo catiado,
the worst for wear,

as if Michael Jackson
had Beat It.

The twelve volunteers
beamed down

in groups of two.
The transporter

estaba fregado, broken.
The ticker tape tardeada

took place in the lab,
no towering skyscrapers,

just hopes
and dreams for the future.

Over the next
year or two,

news trickled in slowly
as the last

of the Google Robotic Reporters
either were destroyed

by the Martian
or succumbed

to mechanical problems.
The Mexicans

were again
strangers in a strange land,

alone in the universe…
For now.

ABOUT THE AUTHOR

Reyes Cárdenas was born on January 6, 1948 in Guadalupe County, Texas. He has lived most of his life in Central Texas, while making a living as a machinist.